Legal & Disclaimer

The information contained in this book and its contents is not designed to replace or take the place of any form of medical or professional advice; and is not meant to replace the need for independent medical, financial, legal or other professional advice or services, as may be required. The content and information in this book has been provided for educational and entertainment purposes only.

The content and information contained in this book has been compiled from sources deemed reliable, and it is accurate to the best of the Author's knowledge, information and belief. However, the Author cannot guarantee its accuracy and validity and cannot be held liable for any errors and/or omissions. Further, changes are periodically made to this book as and when needed. Where appropriate and/or necessary, you must consult a professional (including but not limited to your doctor, attorney, financial advisor or such other professional advisor) before using any of the suggested remedies, techniques, or information in this book.

CONTENTS

INTRODUCTION

Cooking on a charcoal grill can be slightly more complicated than using a gas or electric grill, especially if you're new to the game. But we've got you covered! Here are our eight top tips to help you master the art of charcoal grilling.

8 Tips to Help You Master Your Charcoal Grill

Use a Chimney Starter

Chimney starters are a must for charcoal grilling. They will light up to 100 charcoal briquets and get them red hot within 20 minutes, using nothing but a match and a single sheet of newspaper. No more lighter fluid! That means no more exploding lighter fluid or food that tastes like kerosene.

The best chimney starters are the 6-quart models, and you can find them at hardware stores and home stores everywhere.

Use the Right Amount of Charcoal

Once you've gotten your hands on a chimney starter and you're comfortable using it, everything else seems to fall into place. Especially the question of how much charcoal to use. Your target grill temperatures can be easily reckoned in terms of how full your chimney is.

For high-heat grilling, (450 to 550 F, which is ideal for grilling steaks and thin cuts of meat), you want a full chimney. For medium heat (350 to 450 F, perfect for chicken pieces, veggies and seafood), 1/2 to 3/4 chimney. And for low heat (250 to 350 F, for grilling pork ribs, whole poultry, larger roasts and smoking), 1/4 chimney.

Oil and Preheat the Cooking Grate

Oiling the cooking grate ensures that your food doesn't stick to the grill. Preheating is just as important. Trying to cook a steak on a cold grill will cause it to spend too long on the grill and overcook. You also won't get those lovely grill marks. For safety, oil the grate before you set it over the hot coals. Here's more about taking care of your charcoal grill.

Learn How to Vent

Unlike with a gas grill (or your kitchen range), you can't adjust the temperature with a knob or dial on a charcoal grill. But you can control how hot the coals on your grill burn by controlling the flow of oxygen, and you do that by opening and closing the vents.

Opening the vents allows more oxygen, which produces a hotter grill. Trimming the vents slows the oxygen, which cools the grill. But don't close them all the way or your fire will suffocate. And make sure your grill isn't full of ash, which can obstruct the vents.

Know the Difference Between Direct vs Indirect Heat

Another way of controlling how quickly your food cooks is by understanding the difference between direct and indirect heat. A certain amount of coals will produce a certain temperature, but your food will cook faster if it is situated directly above those coals as opposed to away from them. This fact leads us to our next tip...

Build a Two-Zone Fire

Once you've mastered this technique, you're well on your way to mastering charcoal grilling. It's simply a matter of loading the charcoal onto one side of the grill and leaving the other side empty.

It'll still be hot on that side, but it will enable you to move items from the hot, direct-heat side, to the cooler, indirect-heat side. The cooler zone will help prevent overcooking and scorching and will allow you, for example, to grill vegetables and steaks at the same time.

Deal With Flare-ups

A two-zone fire will also help you deal with flare-ups caused by fat from a steak or burger dripping onto the coals. Instead of controling flare-ups using a spray bottle, which can blow ash onto your food, simply move the dripping item over to the indirect zone. With no coals directly underneath, the dripping fat won't flare up.

Enhance Flavor with Wood

The last step on your way to becoming a master of charcoal grilling is incorporating wood. Whether you're doing a full smoke or a true low-temperature barbecue, or you simply want to add some smoke flavor to your grilled items, wood is the key.

Hickory, mesquite, and fruitwoods like apple and cherry, are grillmaster favorites. For smoking and barbecuing, use chunks of dried wood. But for grilling, you can simply add some wood chips on top of your hot coals. Be sure to soak the wood chips first.

SIDES

Grilled Vegetable & Couscous Salad

Servings: 6
Cooking Time: 30 Minutes

Ingredients:

- 1 small zucchini, halved
- 1 small yellow squash, halved
- 1/2 red onion
- 6 sun-dried tomatoes
- 1 tbsp olive oil
- 2 cups uncooked Israeli couscous
- 4 cups vegetable stock, heated
- 4 basil leaves, stacked, rolled, and cut crosswise into thin strips, plus more to garnish
- 2 tbsp coarsely chopped fresh flat-leaf parsley, plus more to garnish
- for the marinade
- 1/4 cup balsamic vinegar
- 1/2 tsp Dijon mustard
- 1 garlic clove, coarsely chopped
- 1/2 cup olive oil
- kosher salt and freshly ground black pepper

Directions:

1. To make the marinade, in a small bowl, whisk together vinegar, mustard, and garlic. Slowly add oil, whisking until combined. Season with salt and pepper to taste.
2. Place zucchini, yellow squash, onion, and sun-dried tomatoes in a shallow dish. Pour half the marinade over the vegetables, toss to coat, and let sit at room temperature for 15 minutes. Cover the remaining marinade and set aside.
3. Preheat the grill to 400°F (204°C) with a cast iron grate installed and a dutch oven on the grate. Remove the vegetables from the marinade and place on the grate around the dutch oven. Close the lid and grill until beginning to soften and char, about 7 to 10 minutes. Transfer the vegetables to a cutting board and cut into bite-sized pieces. Set aside.
4. In the hot dutch oven, heat oil until shimmering. Add couscous, and toast until lightly golden brown, about 2 minutes. Add vegetable stock until couscous is just covered (add hot water if more liquid is needed to cover), close the grill lid, and bring to a boil. Cook until firm to the bite, about 7 to 10 minutes, and drain well.
5. Spoon the couscous into a large serving bowl and add the grilled vegetables, basil, and parsley. Drizzle the reserved marinade over top, and toss well to coat. Serve at room temperature with more basil and parsley to garnish.

Summer Squash & Eggplant

Servings: 6
Cooking Time: 35 Minutes

Ingredients:

- 1 medium yellow squash
- 2 medium zucchini
- 1/4 cup olive oil

- 2 medium yellow onions, sliced into half moons
- 1 medium eggplant, peeled and cut into cubes
- 2 garlic cloves, minced
- 1/2 tsp dried oregano
- 2 cups dry white wine, such as Chardonnay
- 4 tbsp unsalted butter
- kosher salt and freshly ground black pepper
- lemon slices, to serve (optional)

Directions:

1. Preheat the grill to 425°F (218°C) using direct heat with a cast iron grate installed and a dutch oven on the grate. Place squash and zucchini on the grate around the dutch oven, close the lid, and grill until beginning to soften and char, about 5 to 7 minutes. Remove vegetables from the grill and slice into rounds.
2. In the hot dutch oven, heat oil until shimmering. Add onions, and sauté until translucent, about 7 to 8 minutes. Add squash, zucchini, eggplant, garlic, and oregano. Close the lid and sauté until vegetables begin to soften, about 15 minutes. Add white wine, close the grill lid, and simmer until the vegetables have begun to soften and the liquid has reduced by half, about 5 minutes.
3. Remove the dutch oven from the grill and add the butter, stirring until melted. Season well with salt and pepper and a squeeze of lemon. Serve hot with lemon slices (if using).

Broiled Tomatoes And Parmesan

Servings: 4

Cooking Time: 5 Minutes

Ingredients:

- 1/4 cup parmesan, shredded
- 4 roma tomatoes
- 1 Tablespoon olive oil
- 1 tsp red wine vinegar
- Salt & Pepper

Directions:

1. Cut each tomato in half, lengthwise, and brush with olive oil.
2. Grilling:
3. Preheat the grill to 500°F using direct heat with a cast iron grate installed and lower the dome for 2 minutes.
4. Turn the tomatoes, season with vinegar, salt, and pepper and top with parmesan cheese.
5. Lower the dome for an additional 2 minutes or until the cheese melts. Serve warm.

Prosciutto And Pear Bruschetta

Servings: 6

Cooking Time: 5 Minutes

Ingredients:

- 4 oz prosciutto
- 4 oz shaved parmesan cheese
- 1 cup baby arugula
- 1 baguette, sliced 1/2 inch thick
- 1 pear, sliced thin
- 2 Tablespoons olive oil
- 2 Tablespoons high quality balsamic vinegar

Directions:

1. Brush each baguette slice with olive oil and place on a 325°F grill with the dome closed for 5 minutes.
2. Assembly:

3. Remove bread slices and top each with prosciutto, pear slices, parmesan, and baby arugula.
4. Drizzle a few drops of balsamic vinegar over each bruschetta and serve.

Grilled Lemon Garlic Zucchini

Servings: 6
Cooking Time: 5 Minutes

Ingredients:
- 4 zucchini, sliced lengthwise into 1/2 inch slices
- 1/4 cup butter, softened
- 2 tsp parsley, chopped
- 3 cloves garlic, minced
- The zest and juice of 1 lemon

Directions:
1. In a small dish, combine butter, parsley, garlic, lemon zest, and lemon juice.
2. Liberally brush each zucchini slice with the butter mixture.
3. Grilling:
4. Place the zucchini on a 500°F grill and close the dome for 3 minutes.
5. Flip the zucchini and recover with the dome for an additional 2 minutes.
6. Drizzle remaining butter on top of zucchini as it comes off the grill. Serve warm.

Parmesan Zucchini Spears

Servings: 4
Cooking Time: 10 Minutes

Ingredients:
- 4 zucchini, cut in half, then cut into quarters lengthwise

- 1/2 cup parmesan, grated
- 1 tsp Italian seasoning
- 1/2 tsp garlic powder
- Salt and Pepper to taste
- Olive oil for brushing

Directions:
1. Brush each zucchini spear with olive oil and season with salt and pepper.
2. In a small bowl, combine Italian seasoning, garlic powder, and parmesan.
3. Place zucchini spears on a small sheet tray and sprinkle the parmesan over each spear.
4. Grilling:
5. Place the sheet tray on the grid of a 500°F grill.
6. Close the dome and cook for 10 minutes or until the parmesan is golden brown. Serve warm.

Corn & Poblano Pudding

Servings: 8
Cooking Time: 30 Minutes

Ingredients:
- vegetable oil, for greasing
- 4 ears of sweet corn, shucked
- 1 poblano pepper, left whole
- 4 large eggs
- 1 cup whole milk
- 1/2 tsp kosher salt
- 1/4 tsp ground nutmeg
- 1/4 tsp ground cayenne pepper
- 2oz (55g) shredded Cheddar cheese

Directions:
1. Preheat the grill to 350°F (177°C) using indirect heat with a standard grate installed. Grease a cast iron skillet with oil.

2. Place corn and pepper on the grate, positioning them around the edges, close the lid, and grill until beginning to soften and char, about 10 minutes. Transfer the vegetables to a cutting board, cut the kernels from the cobs, and seed and dice the pepper.

3. In a large bowl, whisk together eggs, milk, salt, nutmeg, cayenne, and cheese until well combined. Stir in corn kernels and pepper. Pour the mixture into the greased dish and place on the grate. Close the lid and bake until a knife inserted halfway between the center and the outer edge comes out clean, about 20 minutes. Remove the pudding from the grill and serve warm or at room temperature.

Wood-plank Stuffed Tomatoes

Servings: 8
Cooking Time: 20 Minutes

Ingredients:

- 4 beefsteak tomatoes
- 1 cup chopped fresh flat-leaf parsley
- 3⁄4 cup Italian-style breadcrumbs
- 1 cup grated provolone
- 1⁄4 tsp ground black pepper
- 1 tsp unsalted butter, softened
- 2 tbsp extra virgin olive oil

Directions:

1. Place a 4 x 9in (10 x 23cm) wood plank in a baking dish, cover with cold water, and place heavy cans or stones on the plank to keep it submerged. Soak for 1 to 2 hours.

2. Preheat the grill to 425°F (218°C) using indirect heat with a standard grate installed. Place the wood plank on the grate.

3. Cut tomatoes in half horizontally and hollow out the insides, discarding the seeds and reserving the pulp. Chop the reserved pulp and place in a medium bowl. Add parsley, breadcrumbs, provolone, and pepper, and mix gently to combine. Fill each tomato half with the breadcrumb mixture and top with a drizzle of oil.

4. Flip the plank over, spread butter on the hot side, and arrange tomatoes cut side up on the plank. Place the plank on the grate, close the lid, and cook until the tops are browned and the tomatoes are soft, about 20 minutes. Remove tomatoes from the grill and serve immediately.

Potato, Squash, And Tomato Gratin

Servings: 8
Cooking Time: 35 Minutes

Ingredients:

- 1 lb Yukon gold potatoes, sliced 1/4 inch thick
- 1 lb yellow squash, sliced 1/4 inch thick
- 1/2 cup shredded parmesan cheese
- 5 tomatoes, sliced 1/4 inch thick
- 1/4 cup olive oil, divided
- 2 Tablespoons garlic, minced
- 1 tsp salt
- 1/2 tsp pepper

Directions:

1. Line the bottom of the dutch oven with 2 Tablespoon olive oil.

2. Layer potatoes on the bottom, topped with squash, and topped with tomatoes.
3. Season the tomatoes with salt, pepper, half of the garlic, and half of the parmesan cheese.
4. Repeat with remaining potatoes, squash, and tomatoes.
5. Season with salt, pepper, and remaining garlic.
6. Drizzle with remaining 2 Tablespoon of olive oil and top with remaining parmesan cheese.
7. Grilling:
8. Preheat the grill to 375°F using direct heat with a cast iron grate installed.
9. Place the dutch oven, uncovered, into the grill and close the dome for 30-35 minutes or until the potatoes are cooked through.

Mac And Cheese

Servings: 6
Cooking Time: 60 Minutes

Ingredients:

- 1 lb smoked cheddar cheese, shredded, divided
- 1/4 cup butter
- 2 eggs
- 1/2 lb elbow macaroni
- 3/4 cups evaporated milk
- 1/4 cup Panko breadcrumbs
- 1 tsp salt
- 3/4 tsp dry mustard

Directions:

1. In a large pot of boiling, salted water cook the macaroni according to package directions and drain.

2. In a separate bowl, whisk together the eggs, milk, hot sauce, salt, pepper, and mustard.
3. Grilling:
4. Preheat the grill to 350°F using direct heat with a cast iron grate installed with the dutch oven on the grid.
5. Melt the butter in the dutch oven and place macaroni in the pot. Toss to coat.
6. Stir the egg and milk mixture into the pasta and add half of the cheese.
7. Continuously stir the mac and cheese for 3 minutes or until creamy.
8. Top with remaining cheese and Panko breadcrumbs.
9. Cover the dutch oven, lower the dome, and cook for 20-25 minutes.
10. Serve immediately.

Sweet Potato Fries

Servings: 4
Cooking Time: 25 Minutes

Ingredients:

- 1 tsp fresh thyme, chopped
- 4 large sweet potatoes
- 4 cloves garlic, minced
- 1/4 cup olive oil
- Salt and Pepper

Directions:

1. In a large pot, cover sweet potatoes with cold water and add 2 tsp salt.
2. Bring the water to a boil and cook until the potatoes are soft, but firm, about 15 minutes.
3. In a small sauce pan, heat 2 Tablespoon of the olive oil, garlic, and thyme until fragrant.

4. Cut each sweet potato in half, lengthwise, then in 3 or 4 spears.
5. Brush each spear on cut sides with olive oil, season with salt and pepper.
6. Grilling:
7. Preheat the grill to 425°F using direct heat with a cast iron grate installed and close the dome for 3 minutes.
8. Turn the potatoes and close the dome for an additional 3 minutes or until the sweet potatoes have finished cooking through.
9. Remove the fries and toss with the garlic and thyme oil before serving.

Cowboy Potatoes

Servings: 6
Cooking Time: 60 Minutes

Ingredients:
- 2 lbs Russet potatoes, very thinly sliced
- 1/2 lb bacon, diced
- 2 cups cheddar cheese
- 1 onion, thinly sliced
- 1 tsp salt
- 1/2 tsp pepper

Directions:
1. Preheat the grill to 375°F using direct heat with a cast iron grate installed with the dutch oven on the grid.
2. Add bacon and cook until crisp.
3. Add onion and cook for 3 minutes until it begins to soften.
4. Add sliced potatoes and gently stir to coat the potatoes in the bacon fat. Season with salt and pepper

5. Cover the dutch oven and lower the dome for 40 minutes or until the potatoes are soft.
6. Remove the cover and top with cheese. Replace the cover and allow the dutch oven to sit off the heat for another 2-3 minutes until the cheese is melted.

Wood-plank Loaded Mashed Potatoes

Servings: 16
Cooking Time: 50 Minutes

Ingredients:
- 1lb (450g) red potatoes
- 1lb (450g) Yukon Gold potatoes
- 1 tbsp kosher salt, plus 1 tsp
- 2 strips bacon, diced
- 2 tbsp unsalted butter
- 1/4 cup sour cream
- 1/4 cup heavy cream
- 4oz (113g) shredded Cheddar cheese, plus more for topping
- 4 scallions, thinly sliced, plus more for topping
- freshly ground black pepper

Directions:
1. Place a 4 x 9in (10 x 23cm) cedar wood plank in a baking dish, cover with cold water, and place heavy cans or stones on the plank to keep it submerged. Soak for 1 to 2 hours.
2. Place red potatoes and Yukon Gold potatoes in a large stockpot and add cold water to cover by several inches. Place the pot on the stovetop over high heat, add 1 tsp salt, and bring to a boil. Reduce to a simmer, cover,

and cook until potatoes are fork tender, about 25 minutes. Drain potatoes, reserving 1 cup cooking water.

3. Preheat the grill to 350°F (177°C) using direct heat with a standard grate installed and a cast iron skillet on the grate. Add bacon to the hot skillet, and cook until bacon is crisp and the fat has rendered, about 10 to 15 minutes, stirring occasionally. Transfer the cooked bacon pieces to a plate lined with a paper towel.

4. In a large bowl, combine potatoes, butter, sour cream, heavy cream, Cheddar cheese, scallions, bacon, and 1 tbsp salt. Mash with a potato masher until potatoes have broken down and cheese and sour cream are fully incorporated. If potatoes are too stiff, add some of the reserved cooking water.

5. Place the soaked plank on the grate and allow it to heat for 2 to 5 minutes, then flip it over. Scoop the mashed potatoes onto the heated side of the plank. Top the potatoes with a little Cheddar cheese, close the lid, and cook until cheese has melted and potatoes have browned slightly, about 7 to 10 minutes. Remove potatoes from the grill, sprinkle with scallions, and serve immediately.

Roasted Potatoes

Servings: 20
Cooking Time: 30 Minutes

Ingredients:
- 2lb (1kg) fingerling potatoes, halved
- 1 tbsp chopped fresh cilantro
- 1 tbsp chopped fresh basil
- 1 tbsp chopped scallions, plus more to garnish
- 3 poblano peppers, diced
- ½ cup olive oil
- ½ cup white vinegar
- 3 garlic cloves, minced
- kosher salt and freshly ground black pepper
- 1 cup crumbled queso fresco

Directions:
1. Preheat the grill to 425°F (218°C) using indirect heat with a standard grate installed. In a dutch oven or a disposable aluminum baking dish, combine potatoes, cilantro, basil, scallions, peppers, oil, vinegar, and garlic. Toss well to ensure potatoes are coated in oil and seasonings. Place the dutch oven on the grate and cook until potatoes are fork tender, about 30 minutes.

2. Remove the dutch oven from the grill, season with salt and pepper to taste, and top with the queso fresco and more sliced scallions. Serve immediately.

Grilled Caesar Salad

Servings: 6
Cooking Time: 1 Minutes

Ingredients:
- 2 Tablespoons shredded Parmesan cheese
- 1 Tablespoon olive oil
- 1/4 tsp salt
- 2 heads romaine lettuce, split lengthwise
- 1 cup grated Parmesan cheese
- 2 Tablespoons Dijon mustard
- 3 garlic cloves
- 3 anchovy fillets
- 2 lemons, juiced

- Extra-virgin olive oil
- Kosher salt
- 2 Tablespoons olive oil
- 4 slices day old Italian bread, cubed
- Kosher Salt & Black Pepper to taste

Directions:

1. In a blender or food processor, combine dressing ingredients, minus olive oil and salt.
2. Gradually stream in olive oil until the dressing reaches your desired consistency.
3. Taste and season with salt, if necessary.
4. Grilling:
5. Preheat the grill to 400°F using direct heat with a cast iron grate installed.
6. Toss bread cubes with olive oil, a pinch of salt and a pinch of black pepper and place on a small sheet tray.
7. Place the bread in the grill for 8-10 minutes or until golden brown.
8. Brush cut side of the romaine halves with olive oil and season with salt and pepper.
9. Grill 1 minute over direct heat.
10. Cut the romaine into bite size pieces.
11. Toss lettuce with dressing, croutons, and shredded Parmesan Serve immediately.

Mojito Watermelon

Servings: 8
Cooking Time: 5 Minutes

Ingredients:

- 2 slices watermelon, 1 inch thick
- 1 lime, halved
- 2 Tablespoons mint, julienned
- 1 tsp honey
- 1/2 tsp salt

Directions:

1. Grilling:
2. Place the lime halves, cut side down, on a 500°F grill for 5 minutes.
3. Assembly:
4. Cut the watermelon slices into 8 pie-shaped pieces.
5. Squeeze grilled limes over watermelon.
6. Sprinkle the watermelon with salt, drizzle with honey, and top with mint.

Grilled Paneer

Servings: 6
Cooking Time: 30 Minutes

Ingredients:

- 4 tbsp unsalted butter
- 1 medium white onion, diced
- 3 tbsp chopped fresh ginger
- 1 jalapeño pepper, diced
- 1 tbsp vindaloo curry powder
- 1 tsp kosher salt, divided
- 28oz (800g) can whole peeled tomatoes, preferably fire roasted
- 1/2 tsp ground cinnamon
- 2 tbsp crushed lime leaves
- 3 tbsp honey
- 1/2 cup heavy cream
- 1lb (450g) paneer cheese, thickly sliced
- 8oz (225g) arugula
- 1/4 cup chopped fresh cilantro
- naan bread, to serve (optional)

Directions:

1. Preheat the grill to 425°F (218°C) using direct heat with a cast iron grate installed and cast iron skillet or an all-metal saucepan on the grate. Once hot, add

butter to the skillet, stirring until melted, then stir in onion, ginger, and jalapeño. Sprinkle curry powder and 1/2 tsp salt over top and cook until onions begin to soften and brown, about 5 to 7 minutes, stirring occasionally.

2. Add tomatoes, cinnamon, lime leaves, and honey, pressing tomatoes with a wooden spoon to break them down. Cook uncovered until the sauce thickens and only a little liquid remains, about10 to 15 minutes, stirring occasionally.

3. Transfer the sauce to a blender (or use an immersion blender), and purée on high speed a until smooth, about 1 minute. Wipe the skillet clean and return to the grill. Pour the sauce through a fine mesh strainer back into the skillet. Stir in cream and the remaining 1/2 tsp salt, adding more of each to taste.

4. Place paneer on the grate, close the lid, and cook until the cheese has visible grill marks, about 2 to 3 minutes per side. Cut into large cubes and add to the curry sauce. Gently stir in arugula and half the cilantro. Sprinkle the remaining cilantro over top, and serve immediately with warmed naan (if desired).

Grilled Onions

Servings: 4
Cooking Time: 60 Minutes

Ingredients:
- 4 large sweet onions
- 4 Tablespoons butter
- 1 tsp salt
- 1/2 tsp pepper

Directions:
1. Remove the stem end of each onion and peel the skin away.
2. With a melon baller, remove 1 inch of the core of the onion being careful not to disturb the root end.
3. Place 1 Tablespoon of butter, 1/4 tsp salt, and 1/8 tsp pepper into each onion.
4. Grilling:
5. Wrap the onions in aluminum foil and place on a 225°F grill for 1 hour with the dome closed.
6. Unwrap the onions and serve warm.

Mexican Street Corn

Servings: 6
Cooking Time: 10 Minutes

Ingredients:
- 6 ears corn
- 1/2 cup cotija cheese
- 1 Tablespoon chili powder
- 1 cup mayonnaise
- 1 lime, cut into wedges

Directions:
1. Pull back the husk of the corn and thoroughly remove the silk from each ear of corn.
2. Soak the corn in water for 20 minutes before cooking.
3. Peel back the husks to reveal the corn.
4. Grilling:
5. Preheat the grill to 450°F using direct heat with a cast iron grate installed.
6. Close the dome for 5 minutes, turn the corn, and close the dome for an additional 5 minutes.

7. Remove the corn from the grill. Spread with mayonnaise, sprinkle with chili powder, and coat with cotija cheese.
8. Serve with lime wedges.

Grilled Cabbage With Champagne Vinaigrette

Servings: 6
Cooking Time: 10 Minutes

Ingredients:
- 1 head cabbage
- 2 Tablespoons olive oil
- Salt and Pepper
- 1/2 cup olive oil
- 1/4 cup Champagne vinegar
- 2 Tablespoons capers in brine, drained
- 1 Tablespoon Dijon mustard
- 1 shallot, finely chopped

Directions:
1. Cut the cabbage into 1/2 inch "steaks" from top to root.
2. Brush each side with olive oil and season with salt and pepper.
3. Grilling:
4. Preheat the grill to 425°F using direct heat with a cast iron grate installed and close the lid for 5 minutes.
5. Meanwhile, in a small bowl, combine shallot, mustard, capers, and vinegar.
6. While whisking, stream in olive oil until dressing emulsifies.
7. Flip cabbage steaks and cook on the other side for an additional 5 minutes with the dome closed.
8. Remove cabbage from the grill to a platter and pour dressing over top. Serve warm.

Grilled Endive Salad

Servings: 6
Cooking Time: 2 Minutes

Ingredients:
- 2 cups frisee
- 1/2 cup pecan halves
- 1/4 cup dried cranberries
- 1/4 cup crumbled bacon
- 2 heads endive
- 1 bunch spinach, cleaned and stems removed
- 1/4 cup olive oil
- 2 Tablespoons Dijon Mustard
- 1 Tablespoon honey
- 1 shallot, finely minced
- The juice of 1 lemon
- Kosher salt and fresh cracked pepper to taste

Directions:
1. In a large bowl, combine dressing ingredients. Set aside.
2. Grilling:
3. Split endive down the middle, lengthwise and preheat the grill to 425°F using direct heat with a cast iron grate installed.
4. Remove the endive and slice into half rounds.
5. Toss shredded frisee, sliced endive, spinach, pecans, and cranberries in the dressing and serve immediately.

Alligator Eggs

Servings: 6
Cooking Time: 10 Minutes

Ingredients:
- 8 ounces cream cheese, softened
- 1 cup sharp cheddar cheese

- 12 thin slices bacon
- 6 jalapeños

Directions:

1. Slice jalapeños in half and remove seeds. Set aside.
2. In a small bowl, combine cheddar cheese and cream cheese until mixed.
3. Stuff 2 Tablespoon of the cream cheese mixture into each jalapeño half.
4. Wrap each jalapeño half in one strip of bacon, securing with a toothpick.
5. Grilling:
6. Preheat the grill to 425°F using direct heat with a cast iron grate installed.
7. Place the alligator eggs directly on the grid and close the dome for 10 minutes or until the bacon is crisp. Serve immediately.

Cheesy Tomato Risotto

Servings: 6
Cooking Time: 35 Minutes

Ingredients:

- 1 tbsp unsalted butter
- 1/2 red onion, chopped
- 3 garlic cloves, minced
- 3/4 cup Arborio rice
- 3 cups chicken stock, warmed, plus more as needed
- 2 medium Roma tomatoes, diced small
- 2oz (55g) freshly shredded Parmesan cheese
- 2 scallions, thinly sliced
- 1 tbsp chopped fresh flat-leaf parsley

Directions:

1. Preheat the grill to 350°F (177°C) using indirect heat with a standard grate installed and a dutch oven on the grate. In the hot dutch oven, melt butter. Add onion and garlic, close the grill lid, and cook until barely beginning to soften, about 2 minutes. Add rice, stir, and close the grill lid. Cook until rice is coated with butter and slightly toasted, about 2 to 3 minutes.
2. Add warm stock to the rice 1 cup at a time, stirring often. Add more stock only after the liquid from the previous addition is absorbed. (This will take about 10 minutes each time you add the liquid.) Add tomatoes and cheese, and stir until cheese melts. Add scallions and parsley, and stir until just combined. Remove the dutch oven from the grill and serve immediately.

Corn & Tomato Salsa

Servings: 8
Cooking Time: 10 Minutes

Ingredients:

- 6 ears of corn, shucked
- 1 lime, halved
- 1 avocado, halved
- 1lb (450g) grape tomatoes, quartered
- 1/2 tsp kosher salt, plus more as needed
- 1/2 tsp ground black pepper, plus more as needed
- 2 tsp olive oil
- 4oz (110g) blue cheese, crumbled
- 10 fresh basil leaves, sliced

Directions:

1. Preheat the grill to 425°F (218°C) using direct heat with a cast iron grate installed. Place corn, avocado, and lime on the grate, close the lid, and grill until beginning to soften and char, about 7 to 10 minutes.

Transfer the corn, avocado, and lime to a cutting board. Cut the kernels from the corn and dice the avocado.

2. In a large bowl, gently combine corn, tomatoes, avocado, salt, and pepper. Squeeze the grilled lime over top, drizzle with olive oil, and toss to coat.

3. Top the corn mixture with blue cheese and basil, and toss one final time. Season with salt and pepper to taste. Serve immediately.

Soba Noodle Bowl

Servings: 6
Cooking Time: 30 Minutes

Ingredients:

- 12oz (28g) soba noodles
- 4 scallions
- 2 red bell peppers, left whole
- 1 carrot, peeled
- 1/2 head of napa cabbage
- 1/4 cup chopped hazelnuts
- chopped fresh cilantro, to garnish
- for the sauce
- 1/2 cup peanut butter
- 1/4 cup soy sauce
- 1/3 cup warm water
- 2 tbsp ground ginger
- 1 garlic clove
- 2 tbsp white wine vinegar
- 11/2 tsp honey
- 1 tsp crushed red pepper flakes

Directions:

1. To make the sauce, combine all the sauce ingredients in a blender and purée until smooth. Set aside. (Sauce can be made in advance. Refrigerate in an airtight container and use within 1 week.)

2. Cook the pasta according to the package directions until cooked but still firm to the bite. Drain and rinse well under cold water. Set aside.

3. Preheat the grill to 400°F (204°C) using direct heat with a cast iron grate installed and a cast iron skillet on the grate. Place scallions, peppers, carrot, and napa cabbage around the skillet, close the lid, and grill until beginning to soften and char, about 7 to 10 minutes. Slice peppers and carrots thinly, and shred cabbage.

4. Add the vegetables and noodles to the hot skillet, and stir to combine. Add the sauce, and stir until well incorporated and heated through, about 3 to 4 minutes.

5. Remove the skillet from the grill and top noodles with hazelnuts and cilantro. Serve immediately.

Sweet Potato Bake

Servings: 6
Cooking Time: 20 Minutes

Ingredients:

- 3 cups cooked and mashed sweet potatoes, cooled
- 1/2 cup butter, melted
- 1/2 cup sugar
- 1/2 cup milk
- 1 tsp vanilla extract
- 1/2 tsp salt
- 3 eggs, beaten
- 1 cup brown sugar
- 1/2 cup self-rising flour
- 1 cup chopped pecans

- 4 Tablespoons butter at room temperature

Directions:
1. Line the dutch oven with a liner.
2. In a large bowl, combine souffle ingredients. Pour into the prepared dutch oven.
3. In a separate small bowl, combine brown sugar, self-rising flour, chopped pecans, and room temperature butter until a crumbly mixture forms.
4. Sprinkle the crumb mixture over the sweet potato mixture.
5. Grilling:
6. Preheat the grill to 400°F using direct heat with a cast iron grate installed.
7. Place the dutch oven, uncovered, into the grill for 20-25 minutes or until the top is golden brown.

German Potato Salad

Servings: 8
Cooking Time: 70 Minutes

Ingredients:
- 2lb (1kg) Yukon Gold potatoes, unpeeled and cut into rounds or bite-sized pieces
- 1⁄2lb (225g) thick-cut bacon
- 3⁄4 cup finely chopped yellow onion
- 1⁄3 cup white vinegar
- 1⁄4 cup sugar
- 1 tbsp Dijon mustard
- 1 tsp kosher salt
- 2 tbsp minced chives, to garnish

Directions:
1. Preheat the grill to 350ºF (177°C) using indirect heat with a cast iron grate installed and a cast iron skillet on the grate. Place potatoes on the grate around the skillet,

close the lid, and roast until fork tender, about 45 minutes. Remove potatoes from the grill and set aside.
2. Add bacon to the hot skillet, close the lid, and cook until crisp, about 10 to 15 minutes. Once crisp, transfer to a plate lined with a paper towel and crumble into small pieces. Pour off the rendered fat, reserving 4 tbsp in the skillet.
3. Add onion to the skillet, close the lid, and cook until translucent and beginning to brown, about 4 to 5 minutes. Whisk in vinegar, sugar, mustard, and salt, and stir until thick and bubbly, about 2 to 3 minutes. Add the cooked potatoes, and toss to coat.
4. Remove the skillet from the grill, top with crumbled bacon, and garnish with chives. Serve warm.

Dutch Oven Black Beans

Servings: 6
Cooking Time: 40 Minutes

Ingredients:
- 1 medium yellow onion, peeled and halved
- 1 green bell pepper, left whole
- 2 x 15oz (425g) cans black beans with liquid or 3 cups cooked black beans
- 2 garlic cloves, minced
- 1 tsp ground cumin
- 1⁄2 tsp dried oregano
- 1⁄2 tsp kosher salt
- 1 tsp red wine vinegar
- 1 bunch of fresh cilantro, chopped

Directions:

1. Preheat the grill to 350°F using direct heat with a cast iron grate installed and a dutch oven on the grate. Arrange onions and pepper on the grate around the dutch oven, close the grill lid, and grill until beginning to soften and char, about 5 to 7 minutes. Transfer the vegetables to a cutting board and chop.
2. Add 1/8 cup bean liquid to the dutch oven. Add onion, pepper, and garlic, close the grill lid, and sauté until soft, about 2 minutes. Add beans with the remaining liquid. Stir in cumin, oregano, and salt. Cover the dutch oven with its lid and close the grill lid. Simmer for 15 to 30 minutes.
3. Remove the dutch oven from the grill and stir in the vinegar and cilantro, reserving a bit to sprinkle over top. Serve immediately.

Panzanella

Servings: 6
Cooking Time: 8 Minutes

Ingredients:
- 1/2 cup basil leaves
- 3 Tablespoons capers
- 2 large tomatoes, cut into 1 inch cubes
- 1 baguette, cut into 1 inch slices
- 1 yellow pepper, cut into 1 inch pieces
- 1 English cucumber, cut into 1 inch pieces
- 1/2 red onion, thinly sliced
- Olive oil
- Salt and Pepper
- 2 Tablespoons Dijon mustard
- 1/4 cup Champagne vinegar
- 1/2 cup olive oil
- 1/4 tsp salt
- 1/4 tsp pepper

- 2 cloves garlic, finely minced

Directions:
1. Brush the baguette slices with olive oil and place them on a 425°F grill.
2. Close the dome for 2 minutes, turn the bread, and close the dome for another 2-3 minutes or until the bread is golden brown.
3. Assembly:
4. Cut the toasted bread into 1 inch cubes and set aside.
5. In the bottom of a large bowl, combine dressing ingredients.
6. Add bread cubes, cucumber, tomato, bell pepper, and sliced onion and stir to combine.
7. Set aside at room temperature for 20 minutes before serving.

Dutch Oven Baked Beans

Servings: 16
Cooking Time: 40 Minutes

Ingredients:
- 6 scallions, plus more to garnish
- 1lb (450g) bacon, diced
- 3 garlic cloves
- 4 x 15oz (420g) cans Great Northern beans
- 2 tbsp Chinese five-spice powder
- 1/2 cup chopped fresh cilantro
- 2 tbsp black bean garlic sauce
- 2 tsp ground ginger
- 3 tbsp soy sauce
- 1 cup sweet chili sauce

Directions:
1. Preheat the grill to 400°F (204°C) using indirect heat with a cast iron grate installed and a dutch oven on the grate. Place

scallions on the grate around the dutch oven, close the grill lid, and grill until beginning to char, about 2 minutes. Chop scallions and set aside.

2. Place bacon in the dutch oven, close the grill lid, and cook until crisp, about 15 to 20 minutes, stirring occasionally. Use a slotted spoon to remove bacon from the dutch oven and set aside.

3. Drain all but 2 tbsp bacon fat from the dutch oven. Add scallions and garlic, close the grill lid, and cook until just fragrant, about 1 minute. Add beans, five-spice powder, cilantro, garlic sauce, ginger, soy sauce, and chili sauce, and stir to combine. Place the lid on the dutch oven, close the grill lid, and cook beans until heated through, about 15 minutes.

4. Remove the dutch oven from the grill, and stir bacon into the baked beans. Garnish with sliced scallions, and serve immediately.

Grilled Vegetable Succotash

Servings: 6
Cooking Time: 10 Minutes

Ingredients:
- 3 ears corn, shucked and cleaned
- 1 (9 ounces) package baby lima beans, thawed and rinsed
- 1 large tomato, diced
- 1 zucchini, cut lengthwise into 1/2 inch thick slices
- 1 jalapeño
- Additional olive oil for brushing
- 1/3 cup olive oil
- 1/2 tsp salt
- 1/2 tsp pepper
- 1/4 tsp cumin
- The juice of 2 limes

Directions:
1. Grilling:
2. Brush the corn and zucchini on all sides with olive oil.
3. Place the corn on a 500°F grill and lower the dome for 5 minutes.
4. Turn the corn, place the zucchini on the grill, and lower the dome for an additional 5 minutes.
5. Remove the corn, turn the zucchini and cook for 1 minute more.
6. Assembly:
7. Remove the corn from the cob and dice the cooked zucchini.
8. In a large bowl, combine dressing ingredients.
9. Add lima beans, corn, zucchini, tomato, and jalapeño to the bowl and stir to combine.
10. Serve at room temperature.

Breakfast Casserole

Servings: 6
Cooking Time: 40 Minutes

Ingredients:
- 1 lb bulk pork breakfast sausage
- 1 (16 oz) bag of frozen O'Brien style hash browns
- 1 dozen eggs, beaten
- 1/4 cup grated onion
- 1/4 tsp black pepper
- Hot sauce for garnish

Directions:

1. Preheat the grill to 350°F using direct heat with a cast iron grate installed with the dutch oven on the grid.
2. Brown sausage with onion in the dutch oven.
3. Add hash browns and stir to combine.
4. Add eggs and cover.
5. Lower the dome for 15 minutes or until the eggs are just cooked through.
6. Serve the casserole with hot sauce for garnish.

Grilled Artichokes

Servings: 4
Cooking Time: 7 Minutes

Ingredients:
- 4 large artichokes
- 2 Tablespoons olive oil
- 1 lemon
- Salt and pepper
- 1/2 cup mayonnaise
- 2 Tablespoons lemon juice
- 2 Tablespoons basil pesto
- 1/2 tsp sriracha

Directions:
1. Trim artichokes of their fibrous ends and thorny leaves.
2. Quarter the artichokes and remove the thistle in the middle.
3. Rub all cut ends with half of a lemon to prevent browning.
4. In a large steamer, cook artichokes 45 minutes or until just fork tender.
5. Brush each artichoke with olive oil and season with salt and pepper.
6. Grilling:

7. Preheat the grill to 425°F using direct heat with a cast iron grate installed and close the dome for 3 minutes.
8. Turn the artichokes and close the dome for another 2-4 minutes.
9. Serve with dipping sauce.

Smoked Potato Salad

Servings: 8
Cooking Time: 120 Minutes

Ingredients:
- 4 large baking potatoes
- 4 large eggs, hard boiled and finely chopped
- 2 green onions, finely chopped
- 2 large dill pickles, finely chopped
- 1 rib celery, finely diced
- 1/2 cup mayonnaise
- The juice of 1 lemon
- 1/2 tsp black pepper
- 1/2 tsp celery seed
- 1/2 tsp dried dill

Directions:
1. Scrub the potatoes.
2. Grilling:
3. Place the potatoes alongside meat that is smoking at 225°F.
4. Assembly:
5. When the potatoes are fork tender, chill in the refrigerator for 30 minutes.
6. Peel and cut potatoes into small cubes.
7. In a large bowl, combine dressing ingredients.
8. Add potatoes, eggs, green onion, pickle, and celery to the dressing and gently toss

Ratatouille

Servings: 4
Cooking Time: 30 Minutes

Ingredients:
- 1/2 cup fresh, shredded basil
- 2 cloves garlic, minced
- 2 large tomatoes, chopped
- 1 red bell pepper, chopped
- 1 large eggplant, peeled and cut into 1/2 inch cubes
- 1 onion, sliced thin
- 1/4 cup olive oil
- 1/4 tsp dried oregano
- 1/4 tsp dried thyme
- 1/4 tsp fennel seeds
- 3/4 tsp salt

Directions:
1. Preheat the grill to 350°F using direct heat with a cast iron grate installed with the dutch oven on the grid.
2. Add olive oil to the pot and toast oregano, thyme, and fennel for 1 minute.
3. Add onion and cook for 5 minutes or until the onion is soft.
4. Add remaining vegetables, cover, and lower the dome for 20-25 minutes.
5. Serve topped with basil.

Grilled Sweet Potatoes

Servings: 12
Cooking Time: 20 Minutes

Ingredients:
- 5 tbsp olive oil
- 5 tbsp pure maple syrup
- 3 tbsp kosher salt
- 6 garlic cloves, minced, plus more to serve
- 2 tsp finely chopped fresh thyme leaves
- 1/4 tsp crushed red pepper flakes
- 6 large sweet potatoes, about 3lb (1.4kg) in total, peeled and cut into thick wedges
- 2 tbsp finely chopped fresh flat-leaf parsley

Directions:
1. Preheat the grill to 400°F using direct heat with a cast iron grate installed.
2. In a large bowl, whisk together oil, syrup, salt, garlic, thyme, and red pepper flakes. Add potatoes and toss to coat. Season with more salt (if desired).
3. Place wedges on the grate, being sure to shake off excess liquid, close the lid, and grill until lightly golden brown and just cooked through, about 15 to 20 minutes, turning often.
4. Transfer to a serving bowl and immediately toss with parsley and more minced garlic (if desired). Season with salt to taste.

Baba Ganoush

Servings: 8
Cooking Time: 10 Minutes

Ingredients:
- 2 Tablespoons fresh parsley
- 1 eggplant, sliced into 1/2 inch rounds
- 1 clove garlic
- The juice and zest of 1 lemon
- 2 Tablespoons olive oil
- 2 Tablespoons tahini
- Salt & Pepper

Directions:
1. Brush both sides of each eggplant slice with olive oil and season with salt and pepper.

2. Preheat the grill to 425°F using direct heat with a cast iron grate installed and close the dome for 3-5 minutes.
3. Flip the eggplant and close the dome for another 3-5 minutes.
4. Assembly:
5. Peel the eggplant skins away from the flesh and discard.
6. In a food processor, combine eggplant, tahini, parsley, garlic, lemon zest and lemon juice and puree until smooth.
7. Taste for seasoning and add salt and pepper accordingly.
8. Serve at room temperature with pita chips, pretzels, or raw vegetables.

Lasagna

Servings: 12
Cooking Time: 75 Minutes

Ingredients:

- 2 cups ricotta cheese
- 1 cup mozzarella cheese
- 1/2 cup grated parmesan cheese
- 1 egg
- 1 tsp Italian seasoning
- 2 jars (24 oz) marinara sauce or 1 recipe Bolognese sauce
- 1 package no-boil lasagna noodles

Directions:

1. In a medium sized bowl, combine ricotta, parmesan, Italian seasoning, and egg.
2. In a lined dutch oven, pour 1 cup marinara sauce into the bottom of the pot. Layer noodles, ricotta mixture, and sauce in repeating layers ending with sauce.
3. Grilling:

4. Preheat the grill to 350°F using direct heat with a cast iron grate installed.
5. Cover the dutch oven and place it in the grill for 1 hour.
6. Remove from the grill, uncover, and top with mozzarella cheese.
7. Recover the dutch oven and allow the lasagna to sit for 5 more minutes before uncovering.
8. Allow the lasagna to rest for 10 minutes before serving.
9. Traditional Spanish Paella has rabbit, small clams, and chorizo in it. Cubans use lobster, shrimp, and chicken. This version is a combination of the two but the protein is really a matter of taste.

Thanksgiving Stuffing

Servings: 8
Cooking Time: 45 Minutes

Ingredients:

- 8 ounces bulk breakfast sausage
- 4 cups cornbread, crumbled
- 4 cups sourdough bread, cut in cubes
- 1/2 cup onion, diced
- 1/2 cup celery, diced
- 1/2 cup Granny Smith apple, diced
- 4 Tablespoons butter, softened
- 2 cups chicken broth
- 1 tsp poultry seasoning

Directions:

1. Preheat the grill to 375°F using direct heat with a cast iron grate installed with the dutch oven on the grid.
2. Cook breakfast sausage in the dutch oven until brown.

3. Add onion and celery and cook until soft, about 5 minutes.
4. Add apple and cook an additional 2 minutes.
5. Stir in crumbled cornbread and sourdough bread cubes.
6. Pour chicken broth over mixture and season with poultry seasoning.
7. Dot the top of the stuffing with butter, cover, and lower the dome.
8. Cook the stuffing for 30 minutes. Serve warm.

Cowboy Caviar

Servings: 8
Cooking Time: 10 Minutes

Ingredients:
- 2 ears fresh corn on the cob
- 1 large tomato, finely diced
- 1 bell pepper, finely diced
- 1 jalapeño, very finely chopped
- 1/4 cup bottled Italian salad dressing
- 2 cans black beans, drained and rinsed
- 1 can pinto beans, drained and rinsed

Directions:
1. Place shucked and cleaned ears of corn on a 425°F grill and close the dome for 5 minutes.
2. Turn the corn and close the dome for another 5 minutes before removing and setting aside.
3. Assembly:
4. Carefully cut the corn off the cob and place it in a large bow.
5. Add remaining ingredients and toss to combine.

Campfire Potato Salad

Servings: 10
Cooking Time: 10 Minutes

Ingredients:
- 2lb (1kg) new potatoes, unpeeled
- 1 green bell pepper, left whole
- 1 red bell pepper, left whole
- 1/2 red onion
- 1/4 cup mayonnaise
- 1/4 cup sour cream
- 1 tbsp Dijon mustard
- 3/4 tsp garlic, minced
- 1 tbsp kosher salt
- 1/4 tsp ground black pepper
- 1 tbsp chopped fresh dill
- 2 celery stalks, diced

Directions:
1. Preheat the grill to 425°F (218°C) using direct heat with a cast iron grate installed. Place potatoes, peppers, and onion on the grate, close the lid, and grill until beginning to soften and char, about 7 to 10 minutes, turning once or twice.
2. Remove the vegetables from the grill and let cool slightly. Cut the potatoes into quarters and dice the peppers and onion.
3. In a large bowl, combine mayonnaise, sour cream, mustard, garlic, salt, pepper, and dill. Add potatoes, peppers, onions, and celery to the mayonnaise mixture, and gently combine until the vegetables are evenly coated with the dressing. Taste and adjust the seasoning as needed. Serve warm.

Burnt End Baked Beans

Servings: 6
Cooking Time: 30 Minutes

Ingredients:

- 8 oz bacon, finely diced
- 2 cups "burnt ends" from smoked brisket, finely chopped
- 1/2 cup onion, minced
- 2 cloves garlic, minced
- 1 cup favorite barbecue sauce (we like the Classic Texas Barbecue Sauce)
- 1 cup chicken broth
- 1/4 cup brown sugar
- 2 Tablespoons ketchup
- 1 Tablespoon brown mustard
- 2 (15 oz) cans pinto beans, drained and rinsed

Directions:

1. Preheat the grill to 350°F using direct heat with a cast iron grate installed with the dutch oven on the grid.
2. Add the bacon to the dutch oven and cook until crisp.
3. Add onion and garlic and cook 1 minute more.
4. Add remaining ingredients, stir to combine.
5. Cover and lower the dome for 1 hour. Serve hot.

POULTRY

Bou Lentil Turkey Burgers

Servings:6
Cooking Time: 20 Minutes

Ingredients:

- 1 lb ground turkey (very cold)
- Red Split Lentils, prepared
- ½ tsp salt
- ½ tsp black pepper
- Bou Java Rub (optional for seasoning)
- ½ cup red split lentils (soaked for 3 hours)
- 1 BOU Beef or Chicken Broth Cube
- 1 cup water
- 2 BOU Chicken Bouillon Cubes
- ¼ cup espresso coffee, finely ground
- 2 tbsp lemon zest, finely grated
- ½ cup brown sugar
- 2 tbsp sea salt
- 1 tbsp granulated garlic
- 1½ tsp coriander, ground
- 3 tbsp chipotle chili powder
- 2 tbsp black pepper, freshly ground
- 3 tbsp smoked paprika
- 1 tsp roasted cumin, ground
- 1½ tbsp unsweetened cocoa powder
- 1 tsp dry mustard
- 1½ tbsp ancho chili powder

Directions:

1. Thoroughly combine all ingredients. Divide the mixture into 6 equal portions and form into ½ inch thick patties. If desired, season with BOU Java Rub.

2. Grill 6 minutes each side (remember, this is poultry – the internal temperature must get to 165°F).

3. Serve on a grilled whole wheat bun with Dijonnaise, lettuce, tomato and red onion.

4. Crumble the BOU cube in a sauce pan; add the water and blend with a whisk to mix the cube into the water. Add the soaked red lentils; bring to a boil. Lower to a simmer and cook for 4-5 minutes (lentils will be al dente). Pour into a bowl, cover and cool completely under refrigeration.

5. Combine all ingredients in a blender for about 45 seconds.

6. Place into a storage container with a lid; store in a cool dry place

Grilled Vidalia Onion Chicken Peach Skewers

Servings:4
Cooking Time: 10 Minutes

Ingredients:

- 1 large Springer Mountain Farms chicken breast
- 2 Tablespoons fresh lime or lemon juice
- 2 Tablespoons sunflower or canola oil
- Salt and pepper
- ½ Vidalia onion, cut in 1" pieces
- 1 Peach, pitted, cut in 1 "pieces
- Fresh basil
- Bamboo Skewers

Directions:

1. Preheat the grill to 350°F using direct heat with a cast iron grate installed.

2. Soak skewers in water for 30 minutes before using. Slice chicken on bias in thin pieces.Marinate chicken in a bowl with lime or lemon juice, oil, salt and pepper for 10-20 minutes.
3. Weave chicken with peaches and Vidalia onions onto skewers (you can cut chicken and just alternate with peaches and onions).
4. Grill skewers about 4-5 minutes per side. While skewers are cooking melt jelly in microwave. Brush skewers on both sides when you turn them. Garnish with fresh basil cut in ribbons.

Duck And Lemongrass Skewers

Servings:4
Cooking Time: 10 Minutes

Ingredients:
- 1 lb Maple Leaf Farms Ground Duck
- 4 Tbsp finely minced Fresh Lemongrass, tender pale green parts only
- 4 ea Garlic Cloves, finely minced
- 1 cup finely minced Shallots or Yellow Onion
- 1/8 cup finely sliced Scallions
- 2 Tbsp chopped Mint
- 2 tsp Sugar
- 1 tsp Salt
- 1 Tbsp Soy Sauce
- 1 Tbsp Hoisin Sauce
- 1 Tbsp Sriracha
- 8 Skewers (6 inches each), fresh Lemongrass stalks, or disposable wooden chopsticks (soaked in water)
- 1 head Boston Lettuce or Small Green Leaf Lettuce, leaves separated
- Fresh Mint
- Thai or Regular Basil
- shredded Cucumber
- Cilantro
- 2/3 cup Hoisin Sauce
- 1/3 cup Creamy Peanut Butter
- 1/3 cup Warm Water
- 3 Tbsp Fresh Lime Juice
- 1-1/2 Tbsp Soy Sauce
- 2 ea Garlic Cloves, minced
- 1 ea Thai or Serrano Chili, minced (adjust to personal preference)
- 2 tbsp finely grated Carrots, garnish
- 1 tsp chopped Roasted Peanuts, garnish

Directions:
1. Preheat the grill to 350°F using direct heat with a cast iron grate installed.
2. Gently mix together all the ingredients listed except the skewers and lettuce leaves.
3. Form meat mixture into 8 sausage shaped portions (about 1/4 cup each).
4. Gently thread each "sausage" with a lemongrass skewer, or a BGE Flexible Skewer, leaving 2 inches exposed.
5. Grill on kamado grill 6 minutes, turning every two minutes. Remove and place on platter.
6. Place the sauce in a serving bowl and garnish with the shredded carrots and chopped peanuts.
7. Serve with lettuce leaf cups, garnish and sauce .
8. Place the kebab in the lettuce cup, add garnish, remove the lemongrass skewer and dip in sauce.
9. Mix together all ingredients except the carrots and chopped peanuts in a bowl.

Adjust consistency with more warm water if necessary.

10. Refrigerate for at least 1 hour.

Bacon Wrapped Jalapeño Stuffed Chicken Thighs

Servings:6
Cooking Time: 30 Minutes

Ingredients:

- 8 boneless, skinless chicken thighs
- 4 jalapeño peppers
- 8 oz cream cheese
- 16 strips of bacon
- 1 stick of butter
- All-Purpose Rub
- Sweet and Smoky seasoning
- 1 cup salt
- 1/2 cup granulated garlic
- 1/4 cup black pepper

Directions:

1. Preheat the grill to 375°F using direct heat with a cast iron grate installed. If desired, add some pecan chips for some extra smokiness.
2. Remove the thighs from the packaging and place on a cutting board designated for poultry. Trim any excess fat on the thighs and season each side with a hefty dose of Sweet and Smoky seasoning.
3. Cut the jalapeño peppers in half lengthwise and remove the seeds and veins. Fill each half with cream cheese and sprinkle a touch of all-purpose rub on top.
4. Place the stuffed jalapeño peppers cheese side down in the center of each chicken thigh and form the meat around the pepper.

Next, wrap each thigh with 2 strips of bacon.

5. Place the wrapped chicken thigh in a Drip Pan, and top each piece of chicken with a pat of butter. Cook for 30 minutes, until chicken reaches an internal temperature of 165°F.
6. Remove from the kamado grill and let the chicken rest for 8-10 minutes, sprinkle more Sweet and Smoky seasoning on the chicken and spoon some of the butter sauce over the chicken.
7. Serve immediately.
8. Mix all the ingredients together and set aside.

The Perfect Roasted Turkey

Servings:4
Cooking Time: 12 Minutes

Ingredients:

- 1 turkey, cleaned thoroughly
- poultry seasoning
- 1 whole onion cut in half
- 1 stalk celery
- 2 cups chicken broth, wine or water

Directions:

1. Preheat the grill to 325°F using direct heat with a cast iron grate installed. Use a handful of pecan chips for a light, smoky flavor and to provide a deep brown color to the turkey.
2. Spread the seasoning generously over the outside of the bird. Load the bird onto a Vertical Poultry Roaster or Rib and Roasting Rack, then place into a drip pan. Add the onion and celery to the drip pan.

Fill the pan with chicken broth, wine, or water.

3. Cook for 12 minutes per pound until the turkey has reached a safe minimum internal temperature of 165°F throughout the product. Reserve the drippings from the drip pan to make gravy.

Greek Chicken Kebabs

Servings: 4
Cooking Time: 15 Minutes

Ingredients:

- 2 lbs boneless, skinless chicken breasts, cut into large chunks (about 2 inches large)
- Wooden Skewers, soaked for 30 minutes (or Metal skewers)
- 1 recipe Greek Marinade
- 6-ounces Greek style yogurt
- 1/2 cup shredded cucumber
- 1/4 tsp fresh oregano
- 1/4 tsp salt
- 1/8 tsp pepper
- 2 cloves garlic, finely chopped

Directions:

1. Place the chicken breast pieces in a large zip top bag. Pour in Green Marinade.
2. Refrigerate the chicken for as little as 30 minutes or up to 4 hours before cooking.
3. Remove the chicken from the fridge. Thread the chicken onto the skewers without overcrowding them, and set aside.
4. Grilling:
5. Preheat the grill to 400°F using direct heat with a cast iron grate installed.
6. Place chicken skewers on the grids and close the dome for 5 minutes.

7. Turn the skewers and replace the dome for an additional 5-7 minutes or until the chicken is cooked through.
8. Meanwhile, combine ingredients for tzatziki sauce in a small bowl. Serve chicken with warmed pita bread and tzatziki sauce.

Greek Isles Marinated Chicken

Servings:4
Cooking Time: 60 Minutes

Ingredients:

- ¼ cup water
- 2 BOU Chicken Bouillon Cubes
- 1 tbsp Lemon Pepper Seasoning
- 1 tsp Montreal Steak Seasoning
- ½ cup fresh lemon juice
- 1 tbsp oregano, dry
- ½ cup canola oil
- ¼ cup Italian parsley, chopped
- Zest from 1 lemon
- 1 Roasting Chicken (3½ to 3¾ lbs.)
- 3 tbsp oregano leaves, chopped
- 10 oz grape tomatoes, cut in half
- 2 tsp garlic, minced
- ½ cup red onions, sliced thin
- 4 oz crumbled Greek Feta cheese
- 4 oz Kalamata olives, cut in half
- 5 tbsp olive oil
- 2½ tbsp red wine vinegar
- Salt and black pepper to taste
- 5 oz arugula OR Italian parsley

Directions:

1. Combine all ingredients (except for the chicken) in a blender and blend well.
2. Add the chicken breasts to a stainless steel bowl and coat with the marinade. Marinate

for 3 to 4 hours under refrigeration; tossing 2 to 3 times during the marinating time. Or place the chicken into a large 2-gallon resealable bag. Pour the marinade into the bag and seal. Shake to coat the chicken and place under refrigeration (repeat 2 to 3 times during the marinating time).

3. Preheat the grill to 350°F using direct heat with a cast iron grate installed.

4. Remove the chicken from the marinade and allow the excess marinade to drain off. Place the chicken onto a Ceramic Vertical Roaster (fill the roaster with a beer or BOU broth); set the roaster into a Roasting & Drip Pan and place on the cooking grid.

5. Cook to an internal temperature of 165°F in the breast and 175°F in the thigh. Serve with Tomato Feta Salad.

6. Combine all ingredients and toss. Do not over-mix. Place into a serving bowl and serve with Greek Isles Chicken.

Amusement Park Turkey Legs

Servings: 4
Cooking Time: 240 Minutes

Ingredients:
- 2 fresh turkey drumsticks
- 4 cups Turkey Brine
- 2 cups apple or cherry wood chips, soaked in water for 30 minutes

Directions:
1. Submerge drumsticks into the turkey brine for as few as 2 hours and as long as overnight.

2. Remove the drumsticks and discard the brine. Pat the turkey dry.

3. Grilling:

4. Preheat the grill to 250°F using direct heat with a cast iron grate installed. Add soaked, drained wood chips to the burning coals.

5. Put the plate setter in place and place the grid on top.

6. Place the turkey legs on the grid and close the dome for 3-4 hours or until the turkey registers 170°F.

7. Remove the drumsticks and pretend to walk around an amusement park or renaissance fair

Italian Turkey Burger

Servings:4
Cooking Time: 10 Minutes

Ingredients:
- 1 pound ground turkey
- 1 (14.5 ounce) can Red Gold Diced Tomatoes With Basil, Garlic & Oregano, drained very well OR
- 1 (14.5 ounce) can Red Gold Petite Diced Tomatoes With Garlic & Olive Oil, drained very well
- 1 egg, beaten
- ¼ cup bread crumbs
- Salt and black pepper to taste

Directions:
1. Combine ground turkey, Red Gold Tomatoes, egg and bread crumbs in a bowl. Form into patties and season with salt and black pepper.

2. Preheat the grill to 450°F using direct heat with a cast iron grate installed.

3. Place on kamado grill and cook to desired temperature.
4. For added flavor put ¼ cup grated Parmesan cheese into the center of each patty.
5. Serve on toasted Italian bread.
6. Top with a thick pasta sauce (heated). Sprinkle with shredded Italian blend cheese.

Smokey Thai Pulled Chicken Sandwiches

Servings:6
Cooking Time: 92 Minutes

Ingredients:
- 3 lbs boneless skinless chicken thighs
- 1 package of Cobblestone Bread Co.™ Sesame Twist Hamburger Rolls
- 3 tbs chopped cilantro
- quick pickled carrots
- * optional Sriracha sauce
- 3 cups water
- 2 tbs pure cane sugar
- juice of one lime
- 2 tsp Thai fish sauce
- 2 tsp soy sauce
- 1 tbs sea salt
- 1-2 hot peppers (Thai bird or Serrano)
- 2 cloves of garlic
- 1 tbs pure cane sugar
- 2 tsp sea salt
- 1 tsp onion powder
- ½ tsp ground ginger
- ½ tsp garlic powder
- ¼ tsp ground white pepper
- ¼ cup water
- ¼ cup honey
- 1 tbs fresh lime juice
- 2 tbs soy sauce
- 1 tsp Thai fish sauce (add while mixing, do not heat)
- ⅔ pound carrots
- 2½ cups water
- ⅔ cup rice wine vinegar
- 1 tbs pure cane sugar
- 2 tsp sea salt
- 2 tsp fresh grated ginger

Directions:
1. Whisk together ingredients for the brine. Add the chicken thighs, making sure they are fully covered. Place in refrigerator for 2-3 hours.
2. About a half hour before you are ready to grill.Preheat the grill to 280°F using direct heat with a cast iron grate installed.
3. Whisk together the dry rub ingredients. Remove the chicken thighs from brine, and pat dry. Discard brine. Generously coat the chicken with dry rub.
4. Place chicken thighs on the kamado grill. Cook for 1½ hours, flipping once after about 50 minutes. Check temperature occasionally to make sure you are not gout over a maximum of 325°F, damper more narrowly to reduce temperature closer to 280°F.
5. Prepare the Quick Pickled Carrots while the chicken is grilling.
6. When chicken thighs are removed from the kamado grill, set aside to rest and cool a little, then pull the chicken (discard any fatty bits). Mix in chopped fresh cilantro.
7. Mix sauce ingredients, except fish sauce, in a small saucepan over medium-high heat.

Once it comes to a boil, reduce to a simmer. Allow to gently bubble for 2 minutes, then shut off and pour over the pulled chicken. Mix. Add fish sauce and mix again.

8. Place some of the pickled matchstick carrots on the bottom half of each Cobblestone Bread Co.™ Sesame Twist Hamburger Roll. Top with a generous helping of the Thai pulled chicken (squirt on a bit of sriracha sauce if you like) and cover with top of the roll.

9. Peel and trim carrots, then matchstick slice.

10. Whisk together pickling brine ingredients in a deep microwave-safe bowl. Microwave for 2 minutes, then whisk again to ensure salt & sugar are dissolved. Add the carrots. Make sure they are fully covered in the brine.

11. Microwave until the brine come to a quick boil (about 5-6 minutes). Microwave for another minute (you may need to stop it a couple times to avoid boil over). Remove from the microwave and set aside to cool.

12. When the brine has cooled to room temperature, drain. Refrigerate the carrots until ready to go on sandwiches.

Vidalia Onion And Sriracha-glazed Nashville Hot Wings

Servings:4
Cooking Time: 35 Minutes

Ingredients:

- 1 pound whole chicken wings
- 1 tbsp olive oil
- Nashville Hot Seasoning, to taste

- ½ bottle of Vidalia Onion and Sriracha Sauce

Directions:

1. Preheat the grill to 350°F using direct heat with a cast iron grate installed.

2. Separate the flats from the drumettes, discarding the wing tips. Coat with the olive oil and a generous amount of the Nashville Hot Seasoning.

3. Place the wings skin-side down on the grid and cook for 15 minutes. Flip the wings after 15 minutes and cook for another 15-20 minutes, or until the wings measure 175°F internally. Remove the wings and place in a bowl.

4. Pour in ½ bottle of the Vidalia Onion and Sriracha Sauce and stir to coat the wings while they are still hot. Serve and enjoy!

Smoked Wings With Moonshine White Sauce And Ranch Pickles

Servings:12
Cooking Time: 136 Minutes

Ingredients:

- 3 dozen Springer Mountain Farms Chicken Wings

Directions:

1. Preheat the grill to 225°F using direct heat with a cast iron grate installed. Rub 3 dozen wings liberally with BBQ Rub seasoning. Smoke for 1½ to 2 hours or until the internal temperature reaches 165°F or higher.

2. Remove wings from heat and toss with half of the Moonshine White Sauce set aside

and bring the kamado grill up to 425°F. Put wings back on the kamado grill for 8 minutes then flip and cook for another 8 minutes on other side. Toss with remaining Moonshine White Sauce. Serve immediately with Ranch Pickles.

Arroz Con Pollo

Servings: 6
Cooking Time: 60 Minutes

Ingredients:

- 1 large chicken, cut into 8 pieces
- 2 Tablespoon olive oil
- 2 Tablespoon lime juice
- 1 tsp salt
- 1 tsp dried oregano
- 1 tsp ground cumin
- 1/2 tsp freshly ground white pepper
- 1 lb Arborio rice
- 3 cups water
- 1 1/2 cup chicken stock
- 1 cup dry white wine
- 1/4 cup frozen peas, thawed, for garnish
- 2 Tablespoon olive oil
- 1 Tablespoon tomato paste
- 1/2 tsp annatto seeds, or 1/4 tsp saffron threads
- 3 cloves garlic, minced
- 1 small onion, finely chopped
- 1 small red bell pepper, cored, seeded and finely chopped
- 1 small tomato, seeded and diced
- Salt and freshly ground black pepper, to taste

Directions:

1. Wash the chicken and pat dry with paper towels.

2. Mix the oregano, cumin, white pepper, salt and lime juice in a casserole dish. Add the chicken, turning the pieces to cover with the mixture. Let marinate at least 15 minutes.
3. Grilling:
4. Preheat the grill to 400°F using direct heat with a cast iron grate installed with the dutch oven on the grid.
5. Add olive oil and brown the pieces of chicken on all sides.
6. Remove the chicken and drain all but 2 Tablespoon of the fat.
7. Add the onion, bell pepper and garlic to the oil, cook until soft.
8. Add the tomato paste and cook for 1 minute more.
9. Return the chicken to the pan.
10. Add the water, wine, chicken stock, saffron, and season with salt and pepper.
11. Cover with the lid and lower the dome for 30 minutes.
12. Thoroughly wash the rice until the water runs clear.
13. Add rice to the chicken mixture, cover, and lower the dome for 20 more minutes or until the rice is cooked.
14. Garnish with green peas and serve.

Buffa-que Wings

Servings:16
Cooking Time: 40 Minutes

Ingredients:

- 16 whole chicken wings (about 3-1/2 pounds)
- 1/2 cup Tabasco sauce or your favorite hot sauce

- 1/2 cup fresh lemon juice
- 1/4 cup vegetable oil
- 2 tablespoons Worcestershire sauce
- 4 cloves garlic, minced
- 2 teaspoons coarse salt (kosher or sea)
- 1 teaspoon freshly ground black pepper
- 1-1/2 cups wood chips or chunks (preferably hickory or oak), soaked for 1 hour in water to cover, then drained
- 8 tablespoons (1 stick) salted butter
- 1/2 cup Tabasco sauce or your favorite hot sauce
- 4 ounces Maytag Blue cheese
- 1 cup mayonnaise
- 1/2 cup sour cream
- 1 tablespoon distilled white vinegar
- 1/4 cup minced onion
- 1/2 teaspoon freshly ground black pepper
- Coarse salt (kosher or sea; optional)

Directions:

1. Rinse the chicken wings under cold running water and blot them dry with paper towels. Cut the tips off the wings and discard them (or leave the tips on if you don't mind munching a morsel that's mostly skin and bones.) Cut each wing into 2 pieces through the joint.

2. Make the marinade: Whisk together the hot sauce, lemon juice, oil, Worcestershire sauce, garlic, salt and pepper in a large nonreactive mixing bowl. Stir in the wing pieces and let marinate in the refrigerator, covered, for 4 to 6 hours or as along as overnight, turning the wings several times so that they marinade evenly.

3. Make the mop sauce: Just before setting up the grill, melt the butter in a small saucepan over medium heat and stir in the hot sauce.

4. Toss wood chips or chunks in the kamado grill. Preheat the grill to 350°F using direct heat with a cast iron grate installed.

5. When ready to cook, drain the marinade off the wings and discard the marinade. Brush and oil the grid. Place the wings in the center of the hot grate, over the drip pan and away from the heat, and cover the grill. Cook the wings until the skin is crisp and golden brown and the meat is cooked through, 30 to 40 minutes. During the last 10 minutes, start blasting the wings with some of the mop sauce.

6. Transfer the grilled wings to a shallow bowl or platter and pour the remaining mop sauce over them. Serve with Maytag Blue Cheese Sauce and celery for dipping and of course plenty of paper napkins and cold beer.

7. Press the blue cheese through a sieve into a nonreactive mixing bowl.

8. Whisk in the mayonnaise, sour cream, vinegar, onion, and pepper. It's unlikely you'll need salt (the cheese is quite salty already) but taste for seasoning and add a little if necessary. The blue cheese sauce will keep in the refrigerator, covered, for several days.

Thai Stuffed Chicken Drumsticks

Servings: 10
Cooking Time: 40 Minutes

Ingredients:
- 3 lbs chicken drumsticks

- 1/2 lb ground pork
- 6 oz mushrooms, finely chopped
- 4 oz rice vermicelli noodles
- 2 Tablespoons fish sauce
- 1 Tablespoon freshly grated ginger
- 1 Tablespoon minced garlic (about 3 cloves)
- 2 tsp cornstarch
- 1 bunch green onions, finely chopped
- 1 egg
- 1 cup Thai sweet chili sauce
- 2 Tablespoons soy sauce
- 1 tsp fish sauce
- The juice of 1 lime

Directions:

1. Rinse and dry the drumsticks. Using your fingers, gently separate the skin from the meat beginning at the thickest part of the drumstick and leaving the skin attached at the bone.
2. In a large bowl, soak the vermicelli according to the package directions. When they are soft, cut into small pieces.
3. Mix noodles, ground pork, mushrooms, green onion, ginger, garlic, fish sauce, cornstarch, and egg. Divide into equal portions according to the number of drumsticks you intend to cook.
4. Gently work the stuffing under the skin of each drumstick.
5. Grilling:
6. Preheat the grill to 375°F using direct heat with a cast iron grate installed.
7. Place the drumsticks onto the grid and close the dome for 20 minutes.
8. Flip the drumsticks over and continue to cook an additional 20-25 minutes or until

the skin is crispy and the juices of the chicken run clear.
9. Remove from the grid and mix ingredients for the dipping sauce. Serve.

Garfunkel Chicken

Servings:6
Cooking Time: 50 Minutes

Ingredients:
- 1 whole young chicken, 3 to 4 pounds
- 1/2 cup olive oil
- 1 tbsp parsley
- 1 tbsp rubbed sage
- 1 tbsp rosemary
- 1 tsp ground thyme
- 1/2 tsp salt
- 1/2 tsp black pepper

Directions:

1. Remove the backbone from the chicken with either poultry shears or a sharp knife. Turn the chicken over and press down to flatten and break the cartilage in the breast. Rub the entire bird with the olive oil. Mix the herbs and spices together and sprinkle these over the entire bird.
2. Preheat the grill to 350°F using direct heat with a cast iron grate installed. Cook the chicken skin side down for about 15 to 20 minutes until the skin is browned and crispy.
3. Flip the chicken over to bone side down and cook for another 25 to 30 minutes until the internal temperature in the breast is 160°F.

Rosemary Ranch Chicken Kebabs

Servings:4

Cooking Time: 12 Minutes

Ingredients:

- ½ cup olive oil
- ½ cup ranch dressing
- 3 Tbsp Worcestershire sauce
- 1 Tbsp minced fresh rosemary
- 2 tsp salt
- 1 tsp lemon juice
- 1 tsp white vinegar
- ¼ tsp ground black pepper, or to taste
- 1 Tbsp white sugar, or to taste (optional)
- 5 skinless, boneless chicken breast halves – cut into 1 inch cubes

Directions:

1. Preheat the grill to 400°F using direct heat with a cast iron grate installed.
2. In a medium bowl, stir together the olive oil, ranch dressing, Worcestershire sauce, rosemary, salt, lemon juice, white vinegar, pepper and sugar. Let stand for 5 minutes.
3. Add the chicken to the bowl and stir to coat with the marinade. Cover and refrigerate for 30 minutes. Thread chicken onto skewers and discard marinade.
4. Lightly oil the cooking grid. Grill skewers for 8 to 12 minutes, or until the chicken is no longer pink in the center, and the juices run clear.
5. Serve with grilled corn on the cob and grilled veggie skewers.

Smoky Thai Pulled Chicken Sandwiches

Servings:12
Cooking Time: 90 Minutes

Ingredients:

- 3 lbs boneless skinless chicken thighs
- 1 package of Cobblestone Bread Co.™ Sesame Twist Hamburger Rolls
- 3 tbs chopped cilantro
- quick pickled carrots
- * optional Sriracha sauce
- 3 cups water
- 2 tbs pure cane sugar
- juice of one lime
- 2 tsp Thai fish sauce
- 2 tsp soy sauce
- 1 tbs sea salt
- 1-2 hot peppers (Thai bird or Serrano)
- 2 cloves of garlic
- 1 tbs pure cane sugar
- 2 tsp sea salt
- 1 tsp onion powder
- ½ tsp ground ginger
- ½ tsp garlic powder
- ¼ tsp ground white pepper
- ¼ cup water
- ¼ cup honey
- 1 tbs fresh lime juice
- 2 tbs soy sauce
- 1 tsp Thai fish sauce (add while mixing, do not heat)
- ⅔ pound carrots
- 2½ cups water
- ⅔ cup rice wine vinegar
- 1 tbs pure cane sugar
- 2 tsp sea salt
- 2 tsp fresh grated ginger

Directions:

1. Whisk together ingredients for the brine. Add the chicken thighs, making sure they

are fully covered. Place in refrigerator for 2-3 hours.

2. Preheat the grill to 280°F using direct heat with a cast iron grate installed.

3. Whisk together the dry rub ingredients. Remove the chicken thighs from brine, and pat dry. Discard brine. Generously coat the chicken with dry rub.

4. Place chicken thighs on the kamado grill. Cook for 1½ hours, flipping once after about 50 minutes. Check temperature occasionally to make sure you are not gout over a maximum of 325°F, damper more narrowly to reduce temperature closer to 280°F.

5. Prepare the Quick Pickled Carrots while the chicken is grilling.

6. When chicken thighs are removed from the kamado grill, set aside to rest and cool a little, then pull the chicken (discard any fatty bits). Mix in chopped fresh cilantro.

7. Mix sauce ingredients, except fish sauce, in a small saucepan over medium-high heat. Once it comes to a boil, reduce to a simmer. Allow to gently bubble for 2 minutes, then shut off and pour over the pulled chicken. Mix. Add fish sauce and mix again.

8. Place some of the pickled matchstick carrots on the bottom half of each Cobblestone Bread Co.™ Sesame Twist Hamburger Roll. Top with a generous helping of the Thai pulled chicken (squirt on a bit of sriracha sauce if you like) and cover with top of the roll.

9. Peel and trim carrots, then matchstick slice.

10. Whisk together pickling brine ingredients in a deep microwave-safe bowl. Microwave for 2 minutes, then whisk again to ensure salt & sugar are dissolved. Add the carrots. Make sure they are fully covered in the brine.

11. Microwave until the brine come to a quick boil (about 5-6 minutes). Microwave for another minute (you may need to stop it a couple times to avoid boil over). Remove from the microwave and set aside to cool.

12. When the brine has cooled to room temperature, drain. Refrigerate the carrots until ready to go on sandwiches.

Whole Smoked Barbecue Chicken

Servings: 4
Cooking Time: 180 Minutes

Ingredients:

- 2 (2-3 lb) whole chickens
- 1 recipe Basic Barbecue Rub
- 2 cups apple wood chips, soaked for 30 minutes in water

Directions:

1. Generously sprinkle chickens with Basic Barbecue Rub inside and out and set aside.

2. Grilling:

3. Preheat the grill to 225°F using direct heat with a cast iron grate installed.

4. Add wood chips to the charcoal and replace the grid.

5. Place the chickens directly on the grid and close the dome.

6. Cook at 225°F for 3 - 3 1/2 hours or until the internal temperature of the thigh reaches 170°F.

7. Remove the chickens from the grill and allow them to rest for 10 minutes before carving.

8. Serve with your favorite barbecue sauce.

Smoky Grilled Chicken Wings

Servings:6
Cooking Time: 25 Minutes

Ingredients:

- Smoked Paprika Chimichurri
- Marinated Chicken Wings
- ⅔ cup Arugula Leaves, tightly packed
- 1 ⅔ cup Garlic Clove, peeled, finely chopped
- ¼ cup Rosemary Leaves, tightly packed
- 2 cup Italian Parsley Leaves, tightly packed
- ⅔ cup Shallots, finely diced
- 2 tbsp Sage Leaves, tightly packed
- ½ cup Oregano Leaves, tightly packed
- ½ cup Whole Grain Mustard
- 1 ⅔ cup Extra Virgin Olive Oil
- 2 tbsp Smoked Paprika
- 1 tsp Crushed Red Chili Flakes
- ½ cup Red Wine Vinegar
- To taste Sea Salt
- 2 ⅔ cup Water
- ½ cup White Wine Vinegar
- ⅔ cup Lemon Juice
- 2 ½ pounds Chicken Wings
- 1 tbsp Crushed Red Chili Flake
- ¼ cup White Wine Vinegar
- ¾ cup Smoked Paprika Chimichurri
- To taste Fine Sea Salt

Directions:

1. Preheat the grill to 400°F using direct heat with a cast iron grate installed.

2. Place marinated wings on a flat tray and season to taste with sea salt. Place the wings on the kamado grill in a single layer to begin cooking. Allow the skin to begin crisping on one side, then flip and close the lid of the grill to allow the wings to slowly bake as the skin renders crispy. Also closing the lid of the grill will allow the wings to develop that signature smoky flavor that is produced during the cooking process. Maintain a temperature of around 350°F/177°C and check and rotate the wings every 5 minutes to get an even golden brown and crispy skin. The entire process may take anywhere from 20 – 25 minutes. Remove the wings from the heat and place on a wire rack once all the fat is rendered and the skin is evenly crispy and golden brown.

3. Allow to rest for 3 – 5 minutes, then serve.

4. Finely chop all herbs and greens. Combine all finely chopped herbs in a large mixing bowl. Add remainder of the ingredients and mix thoroughly. Reserve finished chimichurri in the refrigerator until ready for use.

5. On a clean cutting board with a sharp knife separate the drumette, flap, and wing tip; discard the wing tips. In a large bowl combine the vinegar, chimichurri, and red chili flakes. Toss the drumettes and flaps in the chimichurri marinade until well coated and allow to sit in the refrigerator for 3½ – 4 hours.

Wickles Brine Blasted Chicken

Servings:8

Cooking Time: 90 Minutes

Ingredients:
- 1 whole chicken (4-5 lb)
- 1 Wickles Jar w/ Brine (pickles eaten or reserved)
- 4 tbsp olive oil
- Rub of your choice
- 1 head garlic (sliced in half lengthwise)
- 3-4 fresh dill sprigs

Directions:
1. Preheat the grill to 325°F using direct heat with a cast iron grate installed.
2. Rise chicken and pat dry. Coat in olive oil and apply rub of your choice to chicken inside and out. Reserve 2 tbsp Wickles brine to combine with oil for basting. Place garlic and dill in a jar with remaining brine. Insert jar into chicken cavity and place on kamado grill.
3. Cook for 1.5 hours. After one hour baste every fifteen minutes with brine mixture until finished.

Grilled Island Chicken

Servings:6

Cooking Time: 12 Minutes

Ingredients:
- 6 boneless, skinless chicken breasts
- 1 (14 oz) can unsweetened coconut milk
- 3 tablespoons minced fresh cilantro
- 1/8 teaspoon ground cinnamon
- 2 tablespoons freshly squeezed lime juice (1 to 2 limes)
- 1 large jalapeño, seeded and minced
- ¼ cup chopped red onion
- ½ cup seeded and chopped tomato
- ½ cup chopped mango
- ¼ cup chopped green bell pepper
- ¼ cup chopped yellow bell pepper
- 1 tablespoon minced jalapeño
- ½ teaspoon kosher salt
- ½ teaspoon chili powder
- 2 tablespoons freshly squeezed lime juice (1 to 2 limes)
- 1 tablespoon honey
- Lime wedges for garnish
- Cilantro sprigs for garnish

Directions:
1. Preheat the grill to 350°F using direct heat with a cast iron grate installed.
2. To make the marinade, using a whisk, mix the coconut milk, cilantro, cinnamon, lime juice and jalapeno in a small bow. Place the chicken breasts in a large shallow dish and pour the marinade over the chicken to cover. Cover the dish with plastic wrap and refrigerate for 2 hours.
3. To make the salsa, toss the onion, tomato, mango, green bell pepper, yellow bell pepper, jalapeno, salt, chili powder, lime juice and honey in a medium bowl. Cover with plastic wrap and refrigerate until ready to use.
4. Remove the chicken breasts from the marinade and discard the marinade. Place the chicken on the Grid and close the lid of the kamado grill. Grill for 10 to 12 minutes per side, until the thermometer reads 160°F/71°C.

5. Place the chicken breasts on plates and top with the salsa. Garnish each plate with lime wedges and a sprig of cilantro.

Greg Bates Bbq Chicken

Servings:8
Cooking Time: 30 Minutes

Ingredients:

- Trimmed chicken Breasts
- 2 cups Dr Pepper
- 2 cups ketchup
- ½ cup no-pulp orange juice
- ¼ cup Worcestershire sauce
- ¼ cup molasses
- 1 tsp ground ginger
- 1 tsp hot paprika
- 1 tsp chipotle Chile powder
- 2 tsp garlic powder
- 2 tsp onion powder
- ½ teaspoon crushed red pepper flakes

Directions:

1. Preheat the grill to 450°F using direct heat with a cast iron grate installed.
2. On your grill over medium high heat for 10 to 15 minutes on each side, brushing the Dr Pepper BBQ sauce on the chicken each time you turn it over. Grill until chicken is cooked through and juices run clear.
3. Mix the Dr Pepper, ketchup, orange juice, Worcestershire sauce and molasses in a saucepan. Season with paprika, ginger, garlic powder, red pepper flakes, chipotle powder and onion powder. Bring the sauce to a boil over high heat, proceed to reduce to medium-low heat and simmer for 15 minutes while stirring occasionally.

4. Use right away on your BBQ chicken, or store in your fridge for about a week! Enjoy.

Jamaican Jerk Chicken Wings

Servings:4
Cooking Time: 20 Minutes

Ingredients:

- 6 scallions, greens part only
- 1 tablespoon finely minced fresh ginger
- 1 teaspoon ground allspice
- 1 tablespoon fresh thyme
- 1 tablespoon dark brown sugar
- ½ cup fresh orange juice
- ¼ cup white vinegar
- ¼ cup soy sauce
- ½ cup olive oil

Directions:

1. Preheat the grill to 350°F using direct heat with a cast iron grate installed.
2. Puree all ingredients in a blender until smooth. Pour over chicken wings. Marinate for about 24 hours. Grill wings until done. Serve hot!

Spicy Bourbon Barrel Bbq Wings

Servings:12
Cooking Time: 150 Minutes

Ingredients:

- 3 dozen Springer Mountain Farms Chicken Wings
- 1 liter bourbon
- 4 cups brown sugar
- 1 yellow onion, chopped
- 2 cups dark molasses

- 1 quart ketchup
- 1 cup Worcestershire Sauce
- ½ cup whole fresh garlic
- ½ cup chopped chipotle peppers
- 1 whole bunch, not chopped thyme
- 3 tablespoon Liquid Smoke
- 1 cup honey
- 2 cups Dijon mustard
- 2 oranges, cut in quarters
- Salt to taste

Directions:

1. Combine all ingredients for the sauce in a large stock box and let simmer on low heat for 2 hours, then remove oranges, thyme, and onions. Blend the sauce until smooth, then pour through a strainer. Toss the chicken in the sauce and drain extra sauce.
2. Preheat the grill to 375°F using direct heat with a cast iron grate installed. Cook for about 30 minutes, turning occasionally, until the internal temperature reaches 165°F or higher.

X Factor Chicken Steaks With Whiskey Grilled Onions

Servings:3
Cooking Time: 32 Minutes

Ingredients:

- Twenty-four 6-inch (15 cm) bamboo skewers, soaked in water for a minimum of 1 hour, or metal skewers, or BGE flexible skewers
- 8 boneless chicken thighs
- 3 + 2 tbsp (90 mL) Bone Dust BBQ Spice
- 1 large red onion, sliced into rings
- 1 large white onion

- 1 large sweet yellow onion (Vidalia or Maui or Texas Sweets)
- Drizzle of olive oil
- Drizzle of Maker's Mark bourbon
- 1 cup (250 mL) your favorite gourmet-style barbeque sauce (I use my Crazy Canuck Sticky Chicken and Rib BBQ Sauce)
- 2 cups (500 mL) kettle-cooked sour cream and onion potato chips
- 2 tbsp (30 mL) chopped fresh chives
- 1⁄2 cup (125 mL) paprika
- 1⁄4 cup (60 mL) chili powder
- 3 tbsp (45 mL) salt
- 2 tbsp (30 mL) ground coriander
- 2 tbsp (30 mL) garlic powder
- 2 tbsp (30 mL) white sugar
- 2 tbsp (30 mL) curry powder
- 2 tbsp (30 mL) hot mustard powder
- 1 tbsp (15 mL) freshly ground black pepper
- 1 tbsp (15 mL) dried basil
- 1 tbsp (15 mL) dried thyme
- 1 tbsp (15 mL) ground cumin
- 1 tbsp (15 mL) cayenne pepper

Directions:

1. Rub chicken with about 3 tbsp (60 mL) Bone Dust BBQ Spice, pressing the spices into the meat. Skewer each thigh with two skewers in an X pattern. This will keep the chicken flat during grilling. Set aside, keeping refrigerated.
2. Preheat the grill to 500°F using direct heat with a cast iron grate installed.
3. Slice the onions into rings and place in a large bowl. Season with about 2 tbsp (30 mL) Bone Dust BBQ Spice, olive oil and a drizzle of bourbon. Mix.

4. Grill onions for 6–8 minutes per side, until lightly charred and tender. Put the onions in a bowl. Drizzle with a little more bourbon. Drizzle in a little bit of your favorite barbeque sauce and set aside, keeping warm.

5. Brush the chicken steaks with a little oil. Grill steaks, starting skin side down, for 6–8 minutes per side, until fully cooked (internal temperature minimum 160°F) and the skin is crisp. Baste with your favorite barbeque sauce after the flip. Remove chicken steaks from the grill. Remove X skewers and set aside until needed.

6. Crush the sour cream and onion potato chips and sprinkle over the grilled onions, add chives and mix it up. Place a mound of grilled onions on top of each grilled chicken thigh and serve.

7. Mix together the paprika, chili powder, salt, coriander, garlic powder, sugar, curry powder, mustard powder, black pepper, basil, thyme, cumin and cayenne. Store in an airtight container in a cool, dry place away from heat and light.

Duck Stir-fry

Servings:4
Cooking Time: 6 Minutes

Ingredients:
- 3 Tbsp vegetable oil
- 2 tsp ginger root, minced
- 2 tsp garlic, minced
- ¼ tsp dried crushed red pepper flakes
- 1 cup each red and green bell peppers, 1" dice
- ¾ cup celery, chopped
- 2 cups duck meat, cut into bite-size pieces
- 1 cup carrots, ⅛" slice
- ¾ cup onion wedges, ¼" separated
- ½ cup whole baby sweet corn, drained, cut in half lengthwise
- ½ cup prepared stir-fry sauce
- 3-4 cups cooked white rice
- 2 tsp sesame seeds, toasted

Directions:
1. Preheat the grill to 550°F using direct heat with a cast iron grate installed.

2. Heat oil in Stir Fry & Paella Pan on kamado grill. Add ginger, garlic and dried peppers. Stir-fry about ½ minute. Add carrots, peppers and celery. Stir-fry about 3 minutes.

3. Add duck meat, onions, corn and sauce. Stir-fry about 2 minutes or until duck is heated.

4. Serve over cooked rice. Garnish with toasted sesame seeds.

Grilled Chicken Flat Bread With Taylor Farms Sweet Kale Salad

Servings:4
Cooking Time: 15 Minutes

Ingredients:
- 1 loaf of ciabatta bread
- 1 boneless, skinless chicken breast
- Savory Pecan Seasoning
- 1 tomato, sliced
- 1 ball of mozzarella, sliced
- 1 Tbsp olive oil
- Salt and pepper to taste
- 1 Taylor Farms Sweet Kale Chopped Kit

Directions:

1. Preheat the grill to 400°F using direct heat with a cast iron grate installed.
2. Season the chicken breast on both sides with the Savory Pecan Seasoning. Place on the grid and cook for 10 minutes per side or until the internal temperature reaches 165°F. Remove the chicken from the grill, slice, and set aside
3. Mix together the Taylor Farms Sweet Kale Chopped Kit and set aside.
4. Slice the ciabatta bread in the middle, lengthwise. Brush the olive oil on the sliced side of the bread and season with the salt and pepper. Place on the bread sliced-side down on the kamado grill for 3-5 minutes, or until desired grill marks appear.
5. Flip the bread and top with the mozzarella. Let cook for 3-5 minutes or until the mozzarella is melting; add tomatoes and cook for 3-5 minutes to desired doneness. Carefully remove from the kamado grill. Add chicken and top with the Taylor Farms Sweet Kale Chopped salad.

Paella

Servings: 6
Cooking Time: 60 Minutes

Ingredients:

- 2 lbs boneless, skinless chicken thighs
- 1 lb bulk chorizo
- 1 lb shrimp, peeled and deveined
- 3 cloves garlic, minced
- 2 lemons, zested
- 1 onion, chopped
- 1 bell pepper, chopped
- 1 quart chicken stock

- 2 cups Arborio rice
- 2 Tablespoons olive oil
- 1 Tablespoon smoked paprika
- 1 tsp dried oregano
- 1/2 tsp salt
- 1/4 tsp crushed red chile flakes

Directions:

1. In a large bowl, combine olive oil, paprika, oregano, salt, and chile flakes
2. Add chicken thighs and stir to combine. Refrigerate while assembling the rest of the ingredients.
3. Grilling:
4. Preheat the grill to 400°F using direct heat with a cast iron grate installed with the dutch oven on the grid.
5. Add chorizo into the dutch oven and cook until browned. Drain all but 2 Tablespoon of the fat.
6. Add chicken to the chorizo and brown on both sides.
7. Add onion and bell pepper and cook until vegetables begin to soften.
8. Add rice and garlic and cook for 3 minutes, until the rice begins to toast.
9. Add chicken stock, cover, and lower the dome for 25-30 minutes or until the rice is cooked through.
10. Remove the lid and allow the rice to toast for an additional 5 minutes. Serve.

Bbq Chicken Cheddar Sandwich

Servings:4
Cooking Time: 35 Minutes

Ingredients:

- 4 slices of Nature's Own 12-Grain Bread

- 2 cups thinly sliced red onion
- 2 teaspoons brown sugar
- ⅛ teaspoon salt
- ¼ teaspoon dried thyme leaves
- 2 cups shredded cooked chicken breast
- 3 tablespoons BBQ sauce
- 2 teaspoons vegetable oil
- 4 (1-ounce) slices reduced-fat deli-style Cheddar cheese

Directions:

1. Preheat the grill to 350°F using direct heat with a cast iron grate installed.
2. Cook chicken 10-12 minutes per side, then toss in bowl with barbecue sauce until evenly coated.
3. Heat oil in   Stir-Fry and Paella Pan.
4. Add onion, brown sugar and thyme; cook 10 minutes or until onion is tender and lightly browned, stirring often. Remove from heat; stir in salt. Set aside.
5. Divide chicken and onion evenly over bread slices; top each with 1 cheese slice. Wrap each open- faced sandwich in heavy-duty foil forming a loose packet; seal all edges.
6. Add to cooking grid for 8 minutes or until heated through. Carefully open foil packets and drizzle with additional barbecue sauce, if desired.

Green Tomato Pizza With Smoked Chicken And Truffle Crema

Servings:8
Cooking Time: 10 Minutes

Ingredients:

- 8 oz (227 g) smoked chicken or turkey, pulled
- ½ red bell pepper, slivered
- 8 oz (227 g) fresh mozzarella cheese, cut into thin slices
- 2 tbsp (30 ml) fresh corn kernels (drain well if using canned)
- 4 or 5 fresh basil leaves, lightly chopped
- 1 cup (240 ml) warm water
- 1 tsp (5 ml) sugar
- 1 tsp (5 ml) active dry yeast
- 3 cups (710 ml) all-purpose flour
- 1½ tsp (8 ml) kosher salt
- ½ tsp (3 ml) dried Italian seasoning (optional)
- 2 tsp (10 ml) olive oil, divided
- 2 tbsp (30 ml) olive oil
- 5 medium green tomatoes
- ½ cup (120 ml) thinly sliced sweet or white onion
- 2 cloves garlic, minced
- 1 tsp (5 ml) kosher salt
- ½ tsp (3 ml) freshly ground black pepper
- 1 tsp (5 ml) sugar
- 1 tbsp (15 ml) white vinegar
- 2 tsp (10 ml) hot red pepper flakes
- ¼ cup (60 ml) fresh basil leaves, roughly chopped
- 1 tsp (5 ml) diced fresh oregano
- ½ cup (120 ml) crema
- 1½ tsp (8 ml) white truffle olive oil

Directions:

1. Run warm water until it is around 110°F, then measure 1 cup (240 ml) into a small bowl. Add the sugar and whisk, then sprinkle in the yeast and let sit until it blooms, 5 to 10 minutes.

2. With a stand mixer, mix together the flour, salt and Italian seasoning. Pour in the water/yeast and blend on low speed until combined. Add 1 tsp (5ml) of the olive oil and continue to blend until a dough forms, then keep mixing for 5 or 6 minutes. Lightly flour a Dough Rolling Mat, dump the dough onto it, and form into a ball. Drizzle the remaining teaspoon of olive oil into a large mixing bowl to coat the inside of the bowl. Transfer the dough ball to the bowl, cover with a damp towel, and let rise until it doubles in size, about 1½ hours.

3. While the dough is rising, prepare the sauce. Use 1 tsp (5 ml) of the olive oil to lightly oil the green tomatoes and char on the kamado grill, then set aside. In a small stockpot over medium heat, heat the remaining olive oil, add the onion and cook until softened, 3 to 4 minutes. Then add the garlic and cook for 2 minutes. Core and chop the tomatoes and add them along with the salt, pepper, sugar, vinegar and red pepper. Cook for 5 minutes, then decrease the heat and simmer for 25 to 30 minutes, stirring occasionally, until the tomatoes are soft. Stir in the basil and oregano, then, using an immersion blender (or food processor), blend until smooth.

4. To make the truffle crema, whisk the crema and truffle oil together. Store covered in the refrigerator until needed.

5. When the dough has risen, place on a lightly floured Dough Rolling Mat and knead 4 or 5 times, then divide into 4 parts. Roll out each piece into a 10 in (25 cm) circle (the thinner the better).

6. To assemble, spoon ½ cup (120 ml) sauce onto each crust and spread with the bottom of a spoon. Lay fresh mozzarella cheese on the pizza, then sprinkle smoked chicken, red bell pepper and fresh corn kernels over the pizzas.

7. Preheat the grill to 600°F using direct heat with a cast iron grate installed. Add a Pizza & Baking Stone. Dust a Pizza Peel with cornmeal, add a pizza, and slide onto the Stone for 5 to 6 minutes, or until the crust is browned and any cheese is melted. Remove and drizzle the Truffle Crema over the pizza, using a fork. Then sprinkle on the basil and serve.

Grillin' Garry's Garlic Parmesan Chicken Legs

Servings:6
Cooking Time: 20 Minutes

Ingredients:
- 6 Chicken Legs
- ½ cup favorite chicken wing rub
- ½ cup butter, melted
- 3 tbsp garlic powder
- ½ cup Parmesan Cheese

Directions:
1. Preheat the grill to 375°F using direct heat with a cast iron grate installed.
2. Season the chicken legs with your favorite chicken wing rub. Mix the butter and the garlic powder together.
3. Add the chicken to the kamado grill. Flip 90° every 5 minutes and baste with garlic butter until an internal temperature of 165°F/74°C.

4. Remove the chicken from the kamado grill and place in a cast iron skillet. Sprinkle with parmesan cheese and cover the pan. Cook for 10-15 minutes, or until the cheese is melted.

Chicken Under A Brick

Servings: 6
Cooking Time: 55 Minutes

Ingredients:

- 1 (4-5 pound) whole chicken
- 1/4 cup Berbere Spice Mix
- 2 Tablespoons olive oil
- 1 garden brick, triple wrapped in aluminum foil

Directions:

1. Spatchcock the chicken by removing the backbone with poultry shears or a sharp knife. Turn the chicken over and press to break the cartilage in the breast.
2. Rub both sides of the chicken with olive oil and sprinkle the spice mix generously over the entire bird. Set aside.
3. Grilling:
4. Preheat the grill to 375°F using direct heat with a cast iron grate installed.
5. Place the chicken, skin side down, on the grid and place the foil covered brick on top. Close the dome for 20 minutes.
6. Remove the brick and flip the chicken bone side down. Replace the brick and close the dome for 25 to 30 minutes or until the internal temperature of the breast and thigh reach 160°F.

7. Remove the brick and set aside to cool. Remove the chicken and allow it to rest for 10 minutes before carving.

The Best Turkey Burger Ever

Servings: 4
Cooking Time: 12 Minutes

Ingredients:

- 1 1/2 pounds ground turkey (a mixture of white and dark meat is best)
- 1/2 cup fresh breadcrumbs
- 1/4 cup shredded onion
- 1/4 cup shredded Granny Smith apple
- 1/2 tsp salt
- 1/4 tsp pepper
- 1 egg, beaten
- 1 clove garlic, grated
- 1/4 cup mayonnaise
- 2 Tablespoon Besto Pesto
- 1/2 tsp sriracha
- 1 cup arugula
- 4 brioche buns
- 1 Granny Smith apple, thinly sliced

Directions:

1. In a large bowl, combine burger ingredients well. Form into 4 patties and refrigerate while the grill comes to temperature.
2. Grilling:
3. Preheat the grill to 450°F using direct heat with a cast iron grate installed.
4. Place turkey burgers onto the grid and close the dome for 3 minutes.
5. Flip the burgers and close the dome for another 3 minutes.

6. Close all of the vents and allow the burgers to sit for 5 minutes more or until the internal temperature reaches 170°F.
7. Stir together aioli mixture.
8. Remove the burgers and serve on a toasted brioche bun with arugula, thinly sliced apple, and a healthy smear of the aioli.

Southwest Turkey Burgers

Servings:4
Cooking Time: 10 Minutes

Ingredients:

- 4 Nature's Own 100% Whole Wheat Sandwich Rolls
- 1/3 cup salsa
- 1/4 cup chopped green onions
- 1 teaspoon dried oregano leaves
- 1/2 teaspoon ground cumin
- 1/4 teaspoon salt
- 1 small ripe avocado, mashed
- 1 tablespoon reduced-fat sour cream
- 1 tablespoon chopped fresh cilantro
- 1 tablespoon lime juice
- 4 lettuce leaves
- 1 pound ground turkey breast
- 4 tomato slices

Directions:

1. Preheat the grill to 450°F using direct heat with a cast iron grate installed.
2. Combine turkey, salsa, green onions, oregano, cumin and salt in large bowl. Shape into four patties. Place patties on grid and grill 4 to 5 minutes per side or until burgers are cooked through.
3. Meanwhile, combine avocado, sour cream, cilantro and lime juice in medium bowl.

Season with salt; set aside. Place lettuce leaf on each roll bottom. Top with burger, tomato slice and avocado mixture.

Braised Chicken Thighs With Mushrooms

Servings: 4
Cooking Time: 60 Minutes

Ingredients:

- 2 lbs chicken thighs, bone in and skin on
- 1 lb mushrooms, thinly sliced
- 1 cup finely chopped onion
- 1 Tablespoon butter
- 1 Tablespoon fresh thyme, chopped
- 1/2 cup white wine
- 1/2 cup chicken broth
- 1/4 cup flour
- 2 Tablespoons olive oil
- Salt and Pepper

Directions:

1. Lightly dredge each chicken thigh in flour and season with salt and pepper.
2. Preheat the grill to 500°F using direct heat with a cast iron grate installed.
3. Place the dutch oven directly on the grid and allow the pot to heat for 5-7 minutes.
4. Pour olive oil into the oven and add chicken thighs, being careful not to crowd the pan.
5. Brown the chicken thighs in batches until they are golden brown on all sides. Remove from the dutch oven and set aside.
6. To the pan, add butter and mushrooms, but do not stir for 2-3 minutes or until the mushrooms begin to brown.
7. Add onions and cook until softened.

8. Return the chicken to the pot and add wine, chicken, broth, and thyme.
9. Cover the dutch oven, reduce the heat of The grill to 350°F and close the dome.
10. Allow the chicken to cook 30-40 minutes or until the internal temperature reaches 170°F. Serve warm.

Smoked Chicken Sandwich With Chipotle Mayonnaise

Servings:12
Cooking Time: 50 Minutes

Ingredients:
- 3 tablespoons of brown sugar
- 1 ½ teaspoons of dry oregano
- 1 ½ teaspoons of onion powder
- 1 ½ teaspoons of garlic powder
- 1 ½ teaspoons of Kosher salt
- 1 teaspoon of ground mustard
- ¼ teaspoon of ground ginger
- ¼ teaspoon of chili powder
- ¼ teaspoon of chipotle powder
- ¼ teaspoon of paprika
- 6 chicken breasts
- 2 cups of mayonnaise
- 3 finely minced chipotle peppers in adobo sauce
- 1 ½ tablespoons of red wine vinegar
- 1 teaspoon of sugar
- Kosher salt to taste
- 3 thinly sliced heirloom tomatoes
- 1 head of butter leaf lettuce, leaves reserved only
- 2 thinly sliced avocados
- 2 cups of packed kale microgreens
- 24 pieces of crisp cooked bacon
- 1 pound on thinly sliced lean ham
- 12 fried eggs to desired amount of doneness
- 12 slices of mozzarella cheese
- 12 slices of pepper jack cheese
- 12 toasted Cobblestone Bread Co.™ Sesame Twist Buns

Directions:
1. Combine all of the herbs and spices in a small bowl and generously add and rub into the chicken breasts on all sides and let it marinate for at least 2 hours and up to 48 hours.
2. Smoke the chicken on the grill for 2 hours or until the chicken reaches an internal temperature of 165°F. Once it is to temperature, wrap each breast in foil and let stand for 30 minutes before slicing.
3. Whisk together all of the ingredients in a medium size bowl until combined and keep cool before serving.
4. Spread a small amount of the chipotle mayonnaise onto the top of a toasted sesame bun and set aside.
5. Next, add a few slices of ham and smoked chicken to the bottom part of a toasted bun along with a slice of each mozzarella and pepper jack and melt under a broiler. Layer on the sliced tomatoes, butter leaf lettuce, crispy bacon, sliced avocado, fried egg, micro greens and the top of the bun with chipotle mayonnaise. Repeat the process 11 more times evenly using up all of the ingredients.

Bbq Chicken Soup

Servings: 8
Cooking Time: 35 Minutes

Ingredients:

- 12 ounces applewood-smoked bacon, diced (about 14 slices)
- 4 tablespoons of your favorite barbecue seasoning
- 1 1/2 pounds tomatoes, chopped (about 4 cups)
- 1 1/2 cups chopped yellow onions
- 1/4 cup minced garlic
- 1 chipotle pepper in adobo
- 12 ounces lite lager beer
- 4 cups chicken stock
- 2 cups ketchup
- 1/4 cup yellow mustard
- 1/2 cup apple cider vinegar
- 1 cup firmly packed light brown sugar
- 2 tablespoons Worcestershire sauce
- 2 cups yellow corn kernels (about 2 ears)
- 1 pound tomatoes, grilled and chopped (about 3 cups)
- 3 cups fresh or frozen lima beans, cooked and drained
- 4 cups chopped Beer-Brined Chicken
- 1 teaspoon freshly ground black pepper

Directions:

1. Preheat the grill to 450°F using direct heat with a cast iron grate installed. Preheat the Dutch Oven on the grid for 10 minutes.
2. Place the bacon in the Dutch Oven, close the lid of the grill, and cook until crisp. Using a slotted spoon, transfer the bacon to a small bowl lined with paper towels and set aside. Reserve the bacon fat in the Dutch Oven.
3. Add the barbecue rub to the bacon fat and cook for 1 minute. Add the tomatoes, onions, garlic, and chipotle and cook for 2 to 3 minutes, until the onions are translucent. Slowly add the beer to the Dutch Oven, stirring with a wooden spoon to deglaze. Add the chicken stock, ketchup, mustard, vinegar, brown sugar, and Worcestershire sauce. Leave the Dutch Oven uncovered, but close the lid of the grill. Simmer for 30 minutes, or until the soup has thickened slightly.
4. Remove the Dutch Oven from the heat. Puree the soup using an immersion blender, or carefully spoon it into the bowl of a food processor fitted with the steel blade, process until smooth, and return to the Dutch Oven. Add the corn, grilled tomatoes, lima beans, chicken, and pepper and stir until completely combined. Serve topped with the reserved bacon pieces.

Stuffed Chicken Breasts With Sundried Tomatoes And Artichokes

Servings: 4
Cooking Time: 40 Minutes

Ingredients:

- 4 boneless, skin on chicken breasts
- 1/2 cup feta cheese
- 1/4 cup frozen spinach, thawed and squeezed dry
- 1/4 cup sundried tomatoes, roughly chopped

- 1 (6 oz) jar marinated artichoke hearts, roughly chopped

Directions:

1. Combine cheese, spinach, tomatoes, and artichokes. Set aside.
2. Using a sharp knife, cut a pocket into the middle of each chicken breast and stuff with the cheese mixture.
3. Season the skin with salt and pepper.
4. Grilling:
5. Preheat the grill to 375°F using direct heat with a cast iron grate installed.
6. Place the chicken breasts on the grid and close the dome for 30-40 minutes or until the chicken is cooked through and the skin is crispy.

Turkey & Wild Mushroom Pot Pie

Servings:4
Cooking Time: 55 Minutes

Ingredients:

- 1½ cups mixed dried wild mushrooms
- 2 Tbsp unsalted butter
- 2 Tbsp olive oil
- 1 cup diced onions
- 1 cup diced carrots
- 1 cup diced celery
- 2 Tbsp minced garlic
- ⅓ cup all purpose flour
- ¼ cup white wine
- 3 cups low-sodium chicken stock
- 1 cup diced potatoes
- 1 tsp minced fresh thyme
- 1 cup frozen green peas
- 2 cups chopped roasted turkey breast

- 1 (9-inch) deep-dish pie shell and 1 pie dough disk
- 1 large egg
- 1 tablespoon water

Directions:

1. Preheat the grill to 375°F using direct heat with a cast iron grate installed. Place the Dutch Oven on the grid to preheat for 10 minutes.
2. Cover the mushrooms with hot water and let rehydrate until needed. Heat the butter and olive oil in the Dutch Oven. Add the onions, carrots, and celery. Close the lid of the kamado grill and cook uncovered for 5 to 6 minutes, until the vegetables are light brown and softened. Add the garlic and stir for 1 minute, then add the flour and stir. Add the wine and cook for 3 minutes.
3. Drain the mushrooms, reserving the liquid. Add the chicken stock and the reserved mushroom liquid to the Dutch Oven and stir well. Add the potatoes. Close the lid of the kamado grill and continue cooking, covered, for 10 minutes, or until the potatoes are cooked through. Add the reserved mushrooms, thyme, peas, and turkey, stir, and cook for 2 to 3 more minutes. Remove the Dutch Oven from the heat and let cool for 15 minutes.
4. Using the Grill Gripper and barbecue mitts, carefully remove the grid and add the platesetter. Replace the grid and raise the kamado grill temperature to 400ºF.
5. Spoon the filling into the pie shell. Roll out the pie dough disk on a lightly floured surface until it is large enough to cover the top of the pie. Unroll the pie dough onto

the pie. Press the top and bottom edges of the dough together and crimp. Using a knife, cut four small slits on the top of the crust. Beat the egg with the water and brush the top with the egg wash.

6. Place the pie on top of the grid and close the lid of the kamado grill. Cook for 30 to 40 minutes, until the dough is light brown and the filling is hot and bubbling. Let rest for 5 minutes before serving.

Smoked Turkey

Servings:8
Cooking Time: 38minutes

Ingredients:
- 12-14 lb. whole turkey
- Sweet and Smoky Seasoning
- Canola oil
- Kosher salt
- ½ orange, cut in half
- ½ onion, cut in half
- 2 sprigs sage
- 2 sprigs rosemary
- 2 sprigs thyme
- 1 whole head of garlic

Directions:
1. Preheat the grill to 225°F using direct heat with a cast iron grate installed.
2. Coat the turkey in canola oil and place on rib rack inside of the roasting pan. Season with salt and sweet and smoky seasoning making sure to season the cavity as well. Put orange, onion, garlic and herbs into the cavity.
3. Smoke in the kamado grill until the internal temperature of the breast meat is 165ºF, the dark meat will be about 185ºF internal temperature. Typically, it is about 30 minutes per lb., between 6 to 8 hours.
4. Let rest for 15 minutes, and serve!

FISH AND SEAFOOD

Grilled Oysters

Servings: 2
Cooking Time: 5 Minutes

Ingredients:

- A dozen fresh oysters (the fresher, closer-to-home you can get the better!)
- 6 Tbsp – a little more than half a package – slow-cultured, Roasted Garlic Basil & Parsley Banner Butter
- 1 lemon, cut into slices or wedges
- 3 Tbsp fresh chives, roughly chopped

Directions:

1. Preheat the grill to 425°F using direct heat with a cast iron grate installed.
2. Take your Roasted Garlic Basil & Parsley Banner Butter out of the fridge and set aside in a small bowl.
3. Carefully shuck the oysters with a small knife (an oyster knife with a rounded tip and a work glove on the hand grasping the oyster is a good choice for novice shuckers). Remove the top, flat shell and discard. Place the rounded (bowl side of the shell) side with the oyster on a Perforated Cooking Grid.
4. Place the Perforated Grid in the kamado grill and then add a half tablespoon of softened Roasted Garlic butter to each oyster.
5. Close the lid and kamado grill for 4 or 5 minutes until the oysters are bubbling (not rubbery). The butter should be completely melted and beginning to caramelize on the shell when done.
6. Remove from the kamado grill and move the oysters to a serving plate with the lemons. Squeeze a few wedges/slices onto the oysters and then scatter the chives across the plate.

Big Game Recipes

Servings: 12
Cooking Time: 70 Minutes

Ingredients:

- 1 tablespoon ancho chile powder
- 1 ½ tablespoons onion powder
- 1 ½ tablespoons garlic powder
- 1 tablespoon thyme, dried
- 1 tablespoon black pepper
- ½ teaspoon cinnamon
- 1 tablespoon all-spice
- 1 tablespoon smoked paprika
- ½ teaspoon nutmeg
- 1 each Falconer's Flight hops pellet
- 1 cup sugar
- ½ cup blood orange juice
- ½ cup chicken stock
- 1 pound chicken wings
- 1 cup Dirty Bird Seasoning
- 1 cup clams, chopped
- 3 cups clam juice
- 2 tablespoons butter
- 9 pieces Tater Tots
- 3 pieces bacon
- 1 cup celery, diced small
- 3 cups heavy cream

- 1 cup pearl onions
- Tabasco to taste
- 2 tablespoons all-purpose flour
- 1 bay leaf
- 1 teaspoon thyme, chopped
- Salt to taste
- Pepper to taste

Directions:

1. Combine all ingredients in a bowl until uniformly mixed. Reserve.
2. In saucepot, add all ingredients. Allow to simmer approximately 10 minutes or until the sugar dissolves. Remove the hops pellet. Reserve.
3. Preheat the grill to 350°F using direct heat with a cast iron grate installed.
4. In a bowl, combine Dirty Bird Seasoning and chicken wings until the wings are uniformly coated.
5. Place seasoned chicken wings on the kamado grill and cook for approximately 20, or until an internal temperature of 165°F is achieved. Turn wings to ensure even cooking.
6. Toss cooked chicken wings in the Blood Orange Gastrique and serve hot.
7. Cut bacon into thirds. Wrap around each individual Tater Tot. Place on a perforated baking sheet and bake for 20 minutes or until bacon is crispy. Next preheat cast iron skillet on your grill.
8. Once hot add butter, then saute onions and celery until tender and slightly translucent. Coat cooked vegetables with all-purpose flour then deglaze with clam juice.
9. Next add clams, heavy cream, tabasco, bay leaf, thyme, salt, and pepper. Allow to simmer for 30 minutes.
10. Add bacon wrapped tater tots just before serving. Serve Hot.

Grilled Lobster Rolls

Servings:4
Cooking Time: 20 Minutes

Ingredients:

- 2 lobster tails, butterflied
- 2½ tbsp mayonnaise
- 1 celery stalk, chopped finely
- 2 tbsp lemon juice
- 1 tbsp of fresh chives
- 1 tsp Tony Chachere's Original Creole Seasoning
- Green onions, chopped
- Nashville Hot Seasoning
- Old Bay Seasoning
- 2 tbsp butter, melted
- ¼ lemon, juiced
- 1 sprig of rosemary
- 2 rolls

Directions:

1. Two hours before cooking, mix together mayonnaise, celery, lemon juice, chives, and Tony's Seasoning. Top with the green onions and refrigerate.
2. Preheat the grill to 400°F using direct heat with a cast iron grate installed.
3. Season the lobster with the Nashville Hot and Old Bay. Cook indirectly until the lobster reaches an internal temperature of 135°F. Transfer to direct cooking and cook

meat side down for two minutes on each side until grill marks show.

4. While the lobster is cooking mix together the butter and the lemon. Base the lobster with the lemon butter mixture using the rosemary sprig as a brush right before removing the lobster from the grill.

5. Toast the rolls on the direct side of the grill. Once the rolls are to the desired doneness remove from the grill. Coat the roll with the premade sauce, stuff with lobster, and serve immediately.

Zesty Cedar Planked Cod

Servings:4
Cooking Time: 15 Minutes

Ingredients:

- 2 5-8 oz cod loin portions
- 1 orange, zested
- 1 lemon, zested
- 1 lime, zested
- 1 tbsp peppercorn medley, ground
- Kosher salt
- Olive oil
- Cedar Grilling Planks

Directions:

1. Preheat the grill to 400°F using direct heat with a cast iron grate installed. Soak the plank in hot water for at least 15 minutes.

2. Rub the cod with olive oil and sprinkle with salt and pepper. Combine the 3 citrus zests and place equal amounts on each piece of cod.

3. Set the cod on the cedar planks and place in the kamado grill. Cook for 10-15 minutes

or until the cod reaches an internal temperature of 125°F.

4. Remove from the kamado grill and serve immediately. Enjoy!

Red Fish Pot Pie

Servings:6
Cooking Time: 40 Minutes

Ingredients:

- Several pounds of cubed red fish
- Potatoes
- Green Beans
- Carrots
- Onions
- Cream of asparagus soup
- French fried onions
- Crescent rolls

Directions:

1. Preheat the grill to 350°F using direct heat with a cast iron grate installed. Meanwhile, inside, boil the potatoes, green beans, carrots and onions.

2. Place cubes of red fish in a greased 9 x 13" pan. Pour the boiled veggies (drained of water) onto the fish. Pour the cream of asparagus soup on top and spread around with a rubber spatula. Layer on the French fried onions.

3. To make dough – roll out the crescent rolls on a clean surface and lay it on top of the other ingredients in the pan.

4. Bake for 30-40 minutes.

5. Remove from grill. You can allow to rest for a few minutes if you like, or consume immediately.

Sesame Prawns

Servings:4
Cooking Time: 10 Minutes

Ingredients:

- 1/4 cup (60 ml) coarsely chopped cilantro
- 2 tbsp (30 ml) chopped fresh mint leaves
- 2 scallions, coarsely chopped
- 1 tbsp (15 ml) chopped fresh ginger
- 2 garlic cloves
- 1/2 tsp (3 ml) red chili flakes (optional)
- 3 tbsp + 1/2 cup (165 ml) fat-free, low sodium chicken broth
- 1 tbsp (15 ml) canola or olive oil
- 1 cup (240 ml) coarsely chopped yellow onion
- 1 medium red bell pepper, diced
- 1 medium yellow bell pepper, diced
- 1 1/2 tsp (8 ml) toasted sesame oil
- 1 lb (450 g) prawns or jumbo shrimp, peeled and deveined
- 1/4 cup (60 ml) low-sodium soy sauce
- Salt and ground black pepper to taste
- 2 tsp (10 ml) toasted sesame seeds, for garnish
- 2 cups (480 ml) cooked wild or brown rice

Directions:

1. Combine the cilantro, mint, scallions, ginger, garlic, chili flakes and 3 tablespoons of the broth in a food processor. Pulse until the mixture is minced but not pureed. Set aside.
2. Preheat the grill to 400°F using direct heat with a cast iron grate installed.
3. In a Stir Fry & Paella Pan, heat the canola oil. Add the onion and bell peppers and cook for 5 minutes, or until the vegetables are just tender. Transfer to a bowl and cover with a towel to retain the heat.
4. Add the sesame oil to the pan. Add the cilantro mixture and cook for about 1 minute, stirring constantly. Add the remaining 1/2 cup to broth and bring to a boil. Add the prawns and soy sauce to the pan and cook for 2 minutes or until the prawns are just cooked. Return the onion/pepper mixture to the pan and stir for 1 minute to heat through.
5. Season with salt and black pepper. Garnish with toasted sesame seeds and serve with warm wild rice.

Creamy Fish And Fennel Bake

Servings:2
Cooking Time: 30 Minutes

Ingredients:

- 1¾ lbs (800 gr) fresh hake or cod fillets, halved
- 1 bulb fennel sliced, feathery tops retained for garnish
- 1½ cups (360 ml) cream
- ½ cup (120 ml) grated parmesan
- 1 teaspoon (5 ml) minced garlic
- Salt and black pepper to taste
- Dill for garnish

Directions:

1. Preheat the grill to 350°F using direct heat with a cast iron grate installed.
2. Arrange the fish fillets and sliced fennel bulb in a dutch oven.
3. In a small mixing bowl combine the cream, parmesan and garlic; pour over the fish and fennel to cover.

4. Place the dutch oven on the cooking grid and bake for 20 to 30 minutes. Season with salt and black pepper to taste. Serve with rice and garnish with dill.

Cold-smoked Rock Shrimp

Servings:6
Cooking Time: 20 Minutes

Ingredients:
- 2 lb. rock shrimp
- 2 qt. ice
- ½ cup rock salt
- 3 sprigs of parsley
- 3 sprigs of tarragon
- 2 radishes, sliced
- Juice/zest of 6 blood oranges
- 1 cup cider vinegar
- ½ cup sugar
- 1 garlic clove, minced
- ½ tsp Aleppo pepper, or chili of your choice

Directions:
1. Preheat the grill to 250°F using direct heat with a cast iron grate installed.
2. Prep the shrimp by placing them on top of a perforated pan or in aluminum foil with a few holes poked through. Place this pan over an ice/rock salt mixture inside a non-perforated pan.
3. Place ½of the herbs on the charcoal and ½ on the cooking grid, then add the pan with the shrimp to the kamado grill and cold-smoke for 20 minutes; the shrimp will not be fully cooked.
4. To serve, place some gastrique in the bottom of a bowl, top with shrimp, add some raw radishes and herbs to the top and enjoy!

5. Mix all the gastrique ingredients together and cook until slightly syrupy. Cool, pour over the shrimp, and let marinate for one hour before serving.

Cedar-plank Salmon

Servings: 4
Cooking Time: 15 Minutes

Ingredients:
- 1½lb (680g) skinless salmon, cut from the thickest part of the fish
- for the brine
- 2⁄3 cup kosher salt
- 2⁄3 cup packed light brown sugar
- 4 tbsp pickling spice
- 8 cups hot water
- for the sauce
- 2 limes
- 2 garlic cloves, minced
- 1 tbsp extra virgin olive oil
- 1 tbsp honey
- 1 tbsp soy sauce
- 1 tsp chopped fresh mint leaves, plus more to garnish
- 1-in (2.5-cm) piece ginger, peeled and grated
- kosher salt and freshly ground black pepper

Directions:
1. Place a 4 x 9in (10 x 23cm) cedar wood plank in a baking dish, cover with cold water, and place heavy cans or stones on the plank to keep it submerged. Soak for 1 to 2 hours.
2. To make the brine, in a large bowl, whisk together salt, brown sugar, pickling spice, and water until salt and sugar have

dissolved. Add ice cubes a few at a time until the liquid is no longer hot. Place the salmon in a large resealable plastic bag and add brine to fully cover. (Any extra brine can be refrigerated and saved for a later use.) Refrigerate for 1 hour.

3. To make the sauce, grate the zest from 1 lime into a small bowl. Squeeze the juice of both limes and add to the bowl, then whisk in garlic, oil, honey, soy sauce, mint, and ginger. Taste and season with salt and pepper.

4. Preheat the grill to 400°F (204°C) using direct heat with a standard grate installed. Remove the cedar plank from the water and pat dry with paper towels. Place the plank on the grate until it starts to crackle and some coloring and charring appear, about 3 minutes, then turn the plank over.

5. Remove salmon from the brine and place it on the hot side of the plank. Generously brush salmon with lime sauce, close the lid, and grill until the fish is just cooked through and slightly flaky but still moist, about 12 to 15 minutes.

6. Remove salmon from the grill, lightly brush with some of the remaining sauce, and garnish with mint leaves. Serve immediately.

Smoked King Salmon

Servings: 8
Cooking Time: 75 Minutes

Ingredients:
- 2lb (1kg) skinless King salmon fillets
- for the brine
- 1⁄2 cup kosher salt
- 1⁄2 cup packed light brown sugar
- 3 tbsp pickling spice
- 6 cups hot water
- for the pesto
- 5 tbsp extra virgin olive oil, divided
- 1⁄4 cup walnut halves
- 2 cups baby arugula, loosely packed
- 1 cup fresh basil leaves, loosely packed
- 3 tbsp freshly grated Parmigiano-Reggiano
- 1 garlic clove
- kosher salt and freshly ground black pepper
- to smoke
- alder or cedar wood chunks

Directions:
1. To make the brine, in a medium bowl, whisk together salt, brown sugar, pickling spice, and water until salt and sugar have dissolved. Add ice cubes until the liquid is no longer hot. Place salmon in a resealable plastic bag, add the brine to cover, and refrigerate for 30 minutes. (Any extra brine can be refrigerated and saved for a later use.)

2. Remove salmon from the brine, pat dry with paper towels, and refrigerate until the surface begins to look dry and feel slightly tacky, about 30 to 60 minutes more.

3. Preheat the grill to 225°F (107°C) using indirect heat. Once hot, add the wood chunks and install a cast iron grate and a cast iron skillet. Place 1 tbsp oil and walnuts in the skillet, close the lid, and cook until they just begin to toast, about 10 to 15 minutes. Remove the walnuts from the grill and let cool.

4. To make the pesto, in a food processor, combine walnuts, arugula, basil,

Parmigiano-Reggiano, and garlic. Process until the mixture is finely chopped. With the processor running, slowly add 4 tbsp oil until well combined. Thin the pesto with 1 tbsp water (if desired). Transfer to a bowl and season with salt and pepper to taste.

5. Place salmon on the grate, close the lid, and cook until the fish reaches an internal temperature of 135°F (57°C) and just begins to flake, about 45 to 60 minutes. Remove salmon from the grill, and serve immediately with the pesto.

Grilled Fish Tacos With Peach Salsa

Servings:4
Cooking Time: 10 Minutes

Ingredients:

- 1 teaspoon cumin
- 1 teaspoon brown sugar
- 1 teaspoon ground coriander
- 2 teaspoons olive oil
- 1½ pounds fresh salmon, halibut, catfish, or your favorite fish
- Corn tortillas
- Lime wedges
- 1½ cups diced fresh peaches
- 1 firm, but ripe avocado, diced
- ¼ cup thinly sliced red onion
- 2 tablespoons chopped fresh cilantro
- ½ small jalapeño, minced
- juice of 1 lime, about 3 tablespoons

Directions:

1. Preheat the grill to 400°F using direct heat with a cast iron grate installed.

2. In a small bowl, combine cumin, sugar, and coriander. Brush fish with olive oil and sprinkle with spice mixture. Grill fish on oiled cooking grid for 3-5 minutes per side until cooked to your liking. Char tortillas on cooking grid, about 10 seconds on each side.

3. Serve tacos with fresh salsa and desired toppings. (cheese, etc.)

4. Combine salsa ingredients in a medium bowl and refrigerate until ready to use.

Grilled Red Snapper With Tamari And Avocado

Servings:4
Cooking Time: 12 Minutes

Ingredients:

- 4 Tablespoon lemon juice
- 1 Tablespoon grated fresh ginger
- 1 Tablespoon fresh minced garlic
- 1 minced shallot
- 1 teaspoon honey
- 1 teaspoon tamari (soy sauce)
- 1 Tablespoon tahini
- 2 lbs. red snapper filets
- 1 large avocado

Directions:

1. Preheat the grill to 400°F using direct heat with a cast iron grate installed.

2. In heavy skillet, combine lemon juice, ginger, garlic, and shallot. Reduce by half over medium heat. In small bowl, combine honey, tamari, ½ cup water and tahini and whisk into lemon mixture. Set aside in warm place.

3. Broil or grill fish for 6 minutes on each side or until done. Serve with the warm sauce and garnish with avocado.

Grilled John Dory

Servings:4
Cooking Time: 20 Minutes

Ingredients:

- 2 whole john dory, 2 lbs. (900g) each, heads removed
- 4 fresh oysters, unopened
- 1 granny smith apple
- 1 green kohlrabi, plus leaf for garnish
- Kohlrabi apple and parsley juice
- Oyster cream
- Borage flowers and sheep's sorrel (or parsley) to garnish
- 1 green kohlrabi
- 2 granny smith apples
- 10 oz. (285 g) parsley
- 1 cup (240 ml) water
- Easythick™ or corn starch to thicken if preferred
- Salt to taste
- 12 unopened oysters
- 2⅛ cups (500 g) cream
- 2 tsp (6 g) agar or gelatin

Directions:

1. Using shears remove all spines from the fish, season with salt and oil. On a mandoline slicer, slice the apple and kohlrabi into very thin slices (allow 3 slices each of apple and kohlrabi per serving). Blanch the slices for 5 seconds in boiling water then refresh in iced water. Drain well.

2. Preheat the grill to 650°F using direct heat with a cast iron grate installed.

3. Cook the fish for 4 minutes per side, then remove to rest for 4 minutes. Place the oysters in their shells onto the grid. Cook for 5 minutes then shuck open, reserving the juice.

4. Put 6 large dots of Oyster Cream into each of 4 bowls. Place 2 slices each of kohlrabi and apple and the kohlrabi leaves. Carefully fillet the grilled fish and remove the skin. Divide the fish between the 4 bowls and top each with a grilled oyster. Add another slice of apple and kohlrabi on top of the fish, then pour in a little of the Kohlrabi, Apple and Parsley Juice. Garnish with herbs and flowers.

5. Blanch parsley in boiling water then refresh in iced water. Blend parsley and the water until very green, strain through a cheesecloth. Juice the apple and kohlrabi. Mix ¼ cup parsley water and ½ cup kohlrabi/apple juice. Season with salt and thicken if desired.

6. Add the oysters and juice to the cream and warm for 15 minutes. Strain through a fine sieve pressing lightly on oysters. Remove the oysters and set aside – you should have about 2½ cups (600 g) cream mixture. Boil with agar or gelatin and allow to set in fridge; blend mixture until smooth and creamy.

Surf Perch

Servings:3
Cooking Time: 10 Minutes

Ingredients:

- 3 Surf Perch, 1-3 pounds each
- Olive oil
- Sea salt and ground black pepper to taste
- Hickory smoking chunks

Directions:

1. Scale and gut the fish, leaving the heads on. Lay them on their side on tinfoil. Pour olive oil over each fish. Sprinkle heavily with ground sea salt and ground pepper.
2. Preheat the grill to 400°F using direct heat with a cast iron grate installed. You want a lot of smoke because the fish will only be cooking for a short amount of time, and they still have their skin on so the smoke will need to penetrate it.
3. Place the fish (still on the tin foil) on the cooking grid and cook until the fish are brown and smoky.
4. The meat will fall off the bones and have a wonderfully smoky flavor. Bon Appetite!

Grilled Shrimp

Servings:4
Cooking Time: 18 Minutes

Ingredients:

- 1 lb shrimp, 16/20 size, peeled and deveined
- ¼ cup olive oil
- ¼ cup lemon juice
- 3 tbsp fresh chopped parsley
- Coarse salt and freshly cracked pepper
- 1 cup dry white wine
- 1 cup shallots minced
- ½ cup unsalted butter, cut into ½ inch cubes, chilled
- 1 tbsp   Citrus & Dill Sauce Seasoning
- 1 tbsp fresh lemon juice

Directions:

1. Preheat the grill to 450°F using direct heat with a cast iron grate installed.
2. In a large, non-reactive bowl, stir together the olive oil, lemon juice, parsley, salt and black pepper. Add shrimp and toss to coat. Marinate in the refrigerator for 30 minutes.
3. For the sauce: In a small saucepan, heat the wine and shallots over medium-high heat until reduced to 2 tablespoons, about 12-15 minutes. Turn off the heat and gradually add each cube of butter into the reduction, whisking after each
4. addition. Add the Citrus & Dill Seasoning, and season with salt as desired. Whisk in the lemon juice and set sauce aside.
5. Place the shrimp on a lightly oiled Perforated Cooking Grid and cook for 2 to 3 minutes per side, or until opaque. Serve the shrimp drizzled with the sauce over quinoa or rice.

Miso Poached Sea Bass

Servings: 4
Cooking Time: 55 Minutes

Ingredients:

- 4 large eggs
- 3 tbsp white miso paste
- 4 sea bass fillets, about 6oz (170g) each, skinned and deboned
- 3 medium red-skinned potatoes

- 12 fresh green beans
- 1 red onion
- 1 medium head of butter lettuce
- 2 large beefsteak tomatoes, sliced
- 16 Kalamata olives, pitted
- 4 tbsp capers
- 2 tbsp chopped fresh flat-leaf parsley
- for the dressing
- 4 garlic cloves, crushed
- 2 tsp Dijon mustard
- 6 tbsp extra virgin olive oil
- 2 tbsp soy sauce
- 2 tbsp white miso
- 3 tbsp rice vinegar
- kosher salt and freshly ground black pepper
- to smoke
- grapevine or apple wood chunks

Directions:

1. Place eggs in a medium saucepan and cover with cold water. Cover the pot with a lid and bring to a boil on the stovetop over high heat. Once boiling, remove the pot from the heat, keep it covered, and let sit for 20 minutes. Drain the water, and set eggs aside to cool. Once cool, peel, halve, and refrigerate until ready to use.
2. To make the dressing, in a small bowl, whisk together garlic, Dijon mustard, oil, soy sauce, miso, and rice vinegar. Season with salt and pepper to taste, and set aside.
3. Preheat the grill to 425°F (218°C) using direct heat with a cast iron grate installed. Add enough water in the dutch oven to cover bass. (Don't add bass to the water yet.) Place the dutch oven on the grate, leave the lid off the dutch oven, and close the grill lid.
4. Once the water starts to simmer, place the wood chunks on the coals. Add miso paste, stirring to dissolve, and then add fish fillets. Leave the lid off the dutch oven, close the grill lid, and cook until cooked through, about 10 minutes per inch of thickness. Remove from the water and set aside.
5. Place potatoes, green beans, and onion on the grate around the dutch oven. Close the lid and grill until charred, about 7 to 10 minutes. Remove the vegetables from the grill, and chop potatoes and onion. Place the vegetables in a medium bowl, add the dressing, and stir to coat.
6. Line a serving platter with the large outer lettuce leaves. Chop the remainder and arrange on the platter. Place tomato slices on one end of the platter, followed by the grilled vegetables. (Don't throw out the dressing from the bowl.) Place fish in the center of the platter. Garnish with sliced hard-boiled eggs, olives, and capers. Sprinkle parsley over top and drizzle the remaining dressing before serving.

Cedar Planked Salmon With Honey Glaze

Servings:4
Cooking Time: 18 Minutes

Ingredients:

- 2 Cedar Grilling Planks
- ½ cup (120 ml) Dijon mustard
- ¼ cup (60 ml) honey
- 1 tbsp (15 ml) balsamic vinegar
- 2 tsp (10 ml) grated orange zest

- 1 tsp (5 ml) minced fresh thyme plus extra for garnish
- 2 tbsp (30 ml) extra-virgin olive oil
- 4 (7 ounce/200 g) salmon fillets, skin on
- Kosher salt and freshly ground black pepper

Directions:

1. Place the planks in a pan, cover with water and let soak for at least one hour and up to eight hours.
2. Preheat the grill to 400°F using direct heat with a cast iron grate installed.
3. Whisk together the mustard, honey, balsamic vinegar, orange zest, and 1 teaspoon thyme.
4. Place the planks on the grid, close the lid of the kamado grill and preheat for 3 minutes. Open the lid and turn the planks over, brush with the olive oil, and place 2 salmon fillets on each plank. Season with salt and pepper and brush generously with the honey glaze. Cook for 12 to 15 minutes for medium.
5. Remove from the heat and garnish with thyme. Pair with a glass of Spellbound Chardonnay.

Scallops With Pea-sto

Servings: 4
Cooking Time: 7 Minutes

Ingredients:

- 1-lb sea scallops
- 2 Tablespoons olive oil
- Salt and Pepper
- Pea-sto
- 1 cup fresh green peas, blanched (you can also use frozen peas that have been thawed)

- 1/2 cup pecorino romano cheese, grated
- 1/4 cup basil leaves
- 1/4 cup mint leaves
- 3/4 tsp salt
- 1/2 tsp pepper
- 1/4 tsp crushed red chile flakes
- Olive oil

Directions:

1. In a food processor, combine peas, basil, mint, salt, pepper, and chile flakes and process until smooth. Add cheese.
2. Add enough olive oil until the pea-sto becomes a sauce-like consistency (about 1/2 cup). Set aside.
3. Grilling:
4. Preheat the grill to 400°F using direct heat with a cast iron grate installed.
5. Brush both sides of the scallops with olive oil and season with salt and pepper.
6. Place scallops on the grill and closer the dome for 3 minutes.
7. Gently flip the scallops and lower the dome for an additional 2-4 minutes.
8. Remove the scallops and pour some of the pea-sto on top.
9. Additional pea-sto can be saved in the fridge for 3 days. (It's delicious on pasta!)

Grilled Lobster Tails With Smoked Caper Cream

Servings:4
Cooking Time: 5 Minutes

Ingredients:

- 4 Atlantic lobster tails
- 1 cup wagyu beef tallow
- 3½ oz (100 g) sage

- 3½ oz (100 g) lemon thyme
- 1 cup (240 ml) heavy cream (or thickened cream)
- 1 pinch sea salt and freshly ground black pepper
- 1 tbsp (15 ml) capers
- ¾ cup (180 ml) white wine vinegar in a spray bottle
- 2 oz (57 g) finger limes (optional)
- 1 lemon, cut into wedges
- 1 bunch parsley

Directions:

1. Using kitchen shears cut the lobster tail and remove the digestive tract that runs through the meat.
2. Preheat the grill to 500°F using direct heat with a cast iron grate installed.
3. As the kamado grill heats, warm the beef tallow in a Sauce Pan to 175°F; add the sage and lemon thyme to infuse. When the kamado grill reaches cooking temperature, add a cast iron skillet to the grid until hot. Pour in the cream and a pinch of salt and pepper. When the cream on the side of the pan turns a light brown color, slowly use the spoon to stir the cream. When the cream is thick and a brown color, remove the pan from the kamado grill, mix in the capers and set aside.
4. Place the lobster tails side up on the cooking grid. Brush the infused beef tallow over the meat. Spritz the meat with white wine vinegar, then close the dome and cook for 3 to 4 minutes.
5. Move the cooked marron or lobster from the kamado grill; top with caper cream, finger

limes, a squeeze of lemon and ice plant or parsley. Add salt and pepper to taste.

Foil Packet Fish Filets

Servings: 4
Cooking Time: 15 Minutes

Ingredients:
- 4 (4 oz each) white fish filets
- 1/2 cup white wine
- 4 Tablespoons butter
- 4 pieces heavy duty foil
- 4 sprigs fresh thyme
- 4 green onions, cut in thirds
- 1 zucchini, julienned
- 1 large carrot, julienned
- 1 clove garlic, minced

Directions:

1. On the bottom of each foil sheet, place zucchini, carrot and onion to create a bed.
2. Place one fish filet on each bed of vegetables and top with garlic, thyme, 1 Tbs of butter, salt and pepper to taste.
3. Gather two sides of the foil together and fold down so the foil is almost touching the food.
4. Roll one side of the foil then pour in 2 Tablespoon of white wine. Close the remaining side. Repeat
5. Grilling:
6. Preheat the grill to 375°F using direct heat with a cast iron grate installed.
7. Place the foil packets on the grid and close the dome for 12-15 minutes or until the fish is cooked through.

Grilled Shrimp And Taylor Farms Tangerine Crunch Wraps

Servings:2
Cooking Time: 6 Minutes

Ingredients:

- 1 lb. large shrimp, peeled and deveined
- Savory Pecan Seasoning
- 4-6 sundried tomato or spinach wraps
- 1 Taylor Farms Tangerine Crunch Chopped Kit
- bamboo skewers, soaked
- Feta cheese, optional

Directions:

1. Preheat the grill to 400°F using direct heat with a cast iron grate installed.
2. Season the shrimp on both sides with the Savory Pecan Seasoning. Skewer the shrimp with the soaked skewers.
3. Place the shrimp on the kamado grill and cook for 3 minutes per side or until the shrimp are pink and firm. Remove from the grill, cool and remove from the skewers.
4. Heat a plancha on the grill, griddle-side up.
5. Mix together the Taylor Farms Tangerine Crunch Chopped Kit. Fill the wrap with the salad, top with shrimp and feta cheese. Roll the wrap to enclose the salad. Heat the wrap on the plancha until you have your desired grill marks. Remove from the kamado grill and serve.

Whole Grilled Snapper In Pipian Sauce

Servings:10
Cooking Time: 76 Minutes

Ingredients:

- 2 whole snappers, cleaned, preferably with heads-on, each about 2 pounds
- Coarse salt, kosher or sea
- Freshly ground black pepper
- Lime, halved, for serving
- 1 sweet onion, peeled and thinly sliced
- 2 garlic cloves, peeled and thinly sliced
- 6 sprigs fresh cilantro
- 1 poblano chile (green or red), seeded and thinly sliced
- Extra virgin olive oil
- 8 fresh tomatillos, husked and rinsed
- 1 poblano pepper
- 3 serrano chiles
- ½ small onion
- 4 cloves garlic, peeled and skewered on a toothpick
- 2 scallions, trimmed
- 2 romaine lettuce leaves, cut into 1-inch slices
- 1 cup hulled pumpkin seeds
- ½ cup fresh cilantro, coarsely chopped
- 2 tbsp fresh flat-leaf parsley, coarsely chopped
- ½ tsp ground cumin
- 1 tbsp fresh lime juice, or more to taste
- 1 ½ cup water, or more as needed
- 2 tbsp extra virgin olive oil
- Sea salt and freshly ground black pepper to taste

Directions:

1. Preheat the grill to 450°F using direct heat with a cast iron grate installed.
2. Generously season the cavities of the fish with salt and pepper, then stuff with the

onion, garlic, cilantro, and chile. Pin the cavities shut with toothpicks.

3. Brush the outside of the fish with olive oil, then make three diagonal, parallel slashes on the top side of each to facilitate even cooking.

4. Arrange the stuffed fish on the grill grate, slashed sides up.

5. Grill the fish until it is tender and the internal temperature is at least 145°F, 30 to 40 minutes, or as needed. Carefully transfer the fish to a platter using a wide spatula.

6. Preheat the grill to 500°F using direct heat with a cast iron grate installed.

7. Brush and oil the grill grate. Grill the tomatillos, poblano, serranos, onion, garlic, scallions, and lettuce leaves until golden brown, 2 to 4 minutes per side. Transfer to cutting board to cool to room temperature, then cut into 1-inch pieces.

8. Toast the pumpkin seeds in a dry cast iron skillet (not nonstick) over medium heat until they begin to brown and pop, 3 minutes. Shake the pan as the seeds cook; do not let them burn. Transfer the seeds to a shallow bowl to cool.

9. Set 3 tablespoons of seeds aside for a garnish, then grind the remaining seeds to a fine powder in a food processor, running the machine in short bursts. Work in 1/2 cup of water.

10. Place the grilled vegetables in a food processor and puree. Work in the cilantro, parsley, cumin, and lime juice. Work in an additional 1 cup water, adding more as needed to obtain a thick but pourable sauce.

11. Heat the olive oil in a large, deep skillet over medium heat. Add the pumpkin seed mixture and cook until dark, thick, and fragrant, about 5 minutes, stirring frequently to prevent splattering or scorching.

12. Stir in the tomatillo mixture and continue cooking the sauce until thick and richly flavored, 15 to 20 minutes, stirring often. Remove the sauce from the heat and taste for seasoning, adding salt to taste and/or more lime juice; the sauce should be highly seasoned. Set the sauce aside and keep it warm.

13. Spoon the Pipian Sauce over or under the fish. Sprinkle with the pumpkin seeds reserved from the sauce recipe. Serve with grilled limes halves for squeezing.

Blackened Grouper Sandwich

Servings: 4
Cooking Time: 12 Minutes

Ingredients:
- 4 skinless grouper fillets, about 6oz (170g) each
- 2 tbsp canola oil
- for the sauce
- 1/4 cup mayonnaise
- 1 1/2 tbsp sweet pickle relish
- 1 tbsp coarse ground mustard
- 1 tbsp ketchup
- for the seasoning
- 2 tsp onion powder
- 2 tsp garlic powder
- 2 tsp dried oregano
- 2 tsp dried basil
- 1 1/2 tsp dried thyme

- 1½ tsp ground black pepper
- 1½ tsp ground white pepper
- 1½ tsp ground cayenne pepper
- 5 tsp paprika
- 3 tsp kosher salt
- to serve
- 4 hoagie rolls
- baby arugula
- tomato slices
- pickle spears

Directions:

1. Preheat the grill to 450°F (232°C) using direct heat with a cast iron grate installed and a cast iron skillet on the grate.
2. To make the sauce, in a medium bowl, combine mayonnaise, relish, mustard, and ketchup. Refrigerate until ready to serve.
3. To make the seasoning, in a small bowl, combine all the seasoning ingredients. Coat the fish fillets on all sides with the seasoning.
4. In the hot skillet, heat oil until shimmering. Place fish fillets in the skillet, close the lid, and cook until fish begin to form a crust, slightly char, and begin to flake, about 3 to 4 minutes per side.
5. Cut rolls in half, place on the grate, close the lid, and grill until grill marks appear, about 2 to 3 minutes.
6. Spread the sauce on the rolls. Place a fillet on each bottom bun, top with arugula and tomato, and close sandwiches. Serve immediately.

Swordfish Steaks With Peach Salsa

Servings: 4
Cooking Time: 15 Minutes

Ingredients:
- 4 swordfish steaks (about 1 inch thick, or 6 ounces)
- 1 Tablespoon olive oil
- Salt & Pepper
- 1/4 cup finely diced red pell pepper
- 1 Tablespoon olive oil
- 1/4 tsp cumin
- 2 peaches, slightly underripe, diced
- 1 jalapeño, seeded and finely chopped
- The juice and zest of 1 lime

Directions:
1. Combine ingredients for the salsa and set aside.
2. Brush both sides of the swordfish steaks with olive oil and season with salt and pepper.
3. Grilling:
4. Preheat the grill to 400°F using direct heat with a cast iron grate installed.
5. Place the steaks directly on the grid and close the dome for 6 minutes.
6. Gently flip the fish and close the dome for another 6-8 minutes or until the fish is firm.
7. Remove from the grid and serve topped with peach salsa.

Grilled Shrimp And Taylor Farms Teriyaki Stir Fry Kit

Servings:4

Cooking Time: 14 Minutes

Ingredients:
- 1 lb. large shrimp, peeled and deveined
- Sweet Kentucky Bourbon Grilling Glaze
- 1 Taylor Farms Teriyaki Stir Fry Kit
- 1 tbsp grapeseed oil

Directions:
1. Thirty minutes to one hour before the cook, marinate the shrimp in the Sweet Kentucky Bourbon Grilling Glaze.
2. Preheat the grill to 500°F using direct heat with a cast iron grate installed. Add the wok to the spander System's platesetter Basket or place directly on the grid.
3. Heat the grapeseed oil in the wok. Add Taylor Farms Teriyaki Stir Fry Kit with the teriyaki sauce. Sauté for about 3-5 minutes stirring frequently. Remove the shrimp from the marinade and add to the wok. Cook for approximately 4 minutes until the shrimp curl and turn pink. Carefully remove the wok from the kamado grill. Divide the stir-fry to bowls and serve.

Red Chili Scallops

Servings:4
Cooking Time: 8 Minutes

Ingredients:
- 3⁄4 cup diced fresh mango
- 1⁄4 cup diced red bell pepper
- 1⁄4 cup diced red onion
- 1⁄4 cup thinly sliced scallions
- 2 tablespoons finely chopped fresh mint
- 1 clove garlic, crushed
- 2 tablespoons freshly squeezed lime juice
- 1 tablespoon extra-virgin olive oil
- 2 teaspoons honey
- 1⁄2 teaspoon kosher salt
- 1⁄4 teaspoon freshly ground black pepper
- 1 pound large sea scallops (12)
- 2 tablespoons Red Chile Rub
- 1 tablespoon cumin seed
- 1 tablespoon coriander seed
- 1 tablespoon red chile flakes
- 1 tablespoon ancho chile powder
- 1 tablespoon kosher salt
- 1 teaspoon sweet paprika
- 1 teaspoon garlic powder

Directions:
1. Set the kamado grill for direct cooking with the Cast Iron Grid.
2. Preheat the grill to 500°F using direct heat with a cast iron grate installed.
3. Using a wooden spoon, combine the mango, bell pepper, red onion, scallions, mint, garlic, lime juice, olive oil, honey, salt, and pepper in a small bowl and stir well. Set aside.
4. Season the scallops generously with the chili rub and place on the Grid. Close the lid of the kamado grill and grill the scallops for about 2 minutes on each side, or until golden and lightly cooked. Transfer the scallops to a platter.
5. To assemble the dish, place 3 scallops on each plate and top with 1⁄4 cup of the salsa. Serve immediately.
6. Toast the cumin seed, coriander seed, and chile flakes in a small skillet on the stovetop for about 5 minutes, or until fragrant. Remove from the heat and allow to cool.
7. Transfer the toasted spices to a spice grinder along with the chile powder, salt, paprika,

and garlic powder. Grind for 15 to 20 seconds, until the spices are completely ground. Transfer to an airtight container until ready to use. Makes ½ cup.

Ricky Taylor's Peri Peri Lobster

Servings:4
Cooking Time: 10 Minutes

Ingredients:
- 4 medium lobster tails
- Juice of 3 lemons
- 1 clove of garlic, minced
- 1 tbsp olive oil
- 3 tbsp salted butter
- ½ tsp Peri Peri powder
- ½ tsp salt
- 1 tsp white wine vinegar
- 2-3 cups cooked white rice

Directions:
1. Preheat the grill to 375°F using direct heat with a cast iron grate installed.
2. For the Peri Peri sauce: Oil a Stir-Fry and Paella Pan with the olive oil; place on the grid and add garlic. Stir the garlic for 1-2 minutes. Add the lemon juice until hot but not boiling. Add the butter, Peri Peri, salt and the white wine vinegar (½ tsp of Peri Peri is quite spicy, adjust that amount to taste).
3. For the lobster: Clean and butterfly the lobster tails, baste with ¼ of the sauce.
4. Place the lobster on the kamado grill meat side down for 8 minutes, basting throughout.

5. Remove the lobsters from the shells and serve over rice; drizzle with remaining Peri Peri sauce.

Shrimp Burgers With Remoulade

Servings: 4
Cooking Time: 10 Minutes

Ingredients:
- 1 lb raw shrimp, peeled & deveined
- 3/4 cups fresh breadcrumbs
- 1/4 cup celery, finely diced
- 1/4 cup green onion, white and light green parts, chopped
- 1/4 cup parsley
- 1 Tablespoon Old Bay Seasoning
- 1 Tablespoon brown mustard
- The juice and zest of 1 lemon
- Olive Oil for brushing
- 1/2 cup mayonnaise
- 2 Tablespoon dill pickle, finely chopped
- 2 tsp prepared horseradish
- 4 hamburger buns
- Shredded lettuce
- Sliced tomato

Directions:
1. In a food processor, combine burger ingredients, minus the breadcrumbs, and process until smooth. Gently fold in breadcrumbs and form into 4 patties. Refrigerate for 20 minutes.
2. Mix remoulade sauce ingredients and refrigerate.
3. Grilling:
4. Preheat the grill to 500°F using direct heat with a cast iron grate installed.

5. Brush both sides of the burgers with olive oil and place directly on the grids. Cover with the dome for 4 minutes.

6. Turn the burgers and cover for another 3 minutes.

7. Close all of the vents and allow the burgers to sit for another 5 minutes or until the burgers reach an internal temperature of 165°F.

8. Place the burgers on bottom buns and top with a dollop of remoulade, sliced tomato, and shredded lettuce.

Smoke-roasted Florida Oysters And Clams

Servings:8
Cooking Time: 10 Minutes

Ingredients:

- 4 tbsp (½ stick) unsalted butter, cut into 4 pieces, divided
- 8 strips bacon, cut into ¼ inch slivers
- 1 bunch scallions, thinly sliced
- 2 jalapenos, seeded and minced
- ¼ cup dill or parsley, minced
- 1 cup white wine
- 16 fresh oysters in the shell
- 16 fresh cherrystone clams in the shell
- Hot sauce, for serving (optional)

Directions:

1. To make the oyster filling, melt 1 tbsp butter in a skillet. Add the bacon, scallions, and jalapenos, and cook over medium heat until the bacon is crisp and the mixture is golden brown. Stir in the dill.

2. Preheat the grill to 500°F using direct heat with a cast iron grate installed.

3. Shuck the oysters, discarding the top shells. Pass the knife under each oyster to loosen it from the bottom shell, but try not to spill any of the juice. Arrange the oysters in a shellfish rack or on a wire rack, again, taking care not to spill the juices. Place a spoonful of the bacon mixture in each shell. Save some for the clams.

4. Place the clams in a grill basket or a disposable aluminum foil pan.

5. Return the remaining bacon mixture to the stovetop. Reheat over medium heat. Add the wine and cook until the wine is reduced. Whisk in remaining butter. Keep warm.

6. Place the oysters on their shellfish rack on the grill grate. Roast for 5 minutes or until just cooked – the bacon mixture will begin to sizzle.

7. Remove the oysters from the grill and replace with the clams in grill basket. Cook for about 3-4 minutes or until the clams open. Discard any clams that fail to open. Toss the clams into the bacon and wine mixture and stir. Season with hot sauce, if desired.

Smoked Scallops

Servings: 4
Cooking Time: 55 Minutes

Ingredients:

- 1/4 tsp ground coriander
- 1/2 tsp ground white pepper
- 1/4 tsp ground cloves
- 3 tbsp sugar
- 2 cups kosher salt
- 3 tbsp chopped fresh cilantro
- 2 tbsp finely grated lemon zest

- 12 large sea scallops
- for the couscous
- 1/2 red bell pepper
- 2 Roma tomatoes
- 1 medium red onion, halved
- 1/4 cup balsamic vinegar
- 1/2 tsp Dijon mustard
- 1 garlic clove, coarsely chopped
- 1/2 cup olive oil, plus 2 tbsp
- kosher salt and freshly ground black pepper
- 11/2 cups dried Israeli couscous
- 3 cups vegetable stock, warmed
- 4 basil leaves, stacked, rolled, and cut crosswise into thin strips
- 1/4 cup chopped fresh flat-leaf parsley
- to smoke
- alder, grapevine, or pecan wood chunks

Directions:

1. In a large bowl, combine coriander, white pepper, cloves, sugar, salt, cilantro, and lemon zest. Bury scallops in the spice mixture, cover with plastic wrap, and refrigerate for 30 minutes.

2. Preheat the grill to 400°F (204°C) using indirect heat with a cast iron grate installed and a dutch oven on the grate. Place pepper, tomatoes, and onion on the grate around the dutch oven and cook until beginning to soften and char, about 7 to 10 minutes. Transfer the vegetables to a cutting board and dice.

3. In a large bowl, whisk together vinegar, mustard, and garlic. Slowly add 1/2 cup olive oil and whisk until combined. Season well with salt and pepper. Add the diced grilled vegetables and toss to coat. Set aside

to marinate at room temperature for 15 minutes.

4. To the hot dutch oven, heat the remaining 2 tbsp oil until shimmering. Add couscous and toast until lightly golden brown, about 2 minutes. Add stock to cover, close grill, and cook uncovered until couscous is cooked but still firm to the bite and the liquid is absorbed, about 10 minutes. Add the cooked couscous to the bowl with the grilled vegetables and toss well to incorporate. Set aside.

5. Convert the grill for smoking by removing the cast iron grate, adding one wood chunk to the hot coals, and installing the heat deflector and a standard grate. Close the top and bottom vents most of the way to reduce the temperature to 225°F (107°C).

6. Remove the scallops from the salt pack, rinse under cold water, and pat dry with paper towels. Place scallops on the grate and smoke until slightly firm and light brown in color, about 20 to 30 minutes. Just before serving, scatter the basil and parsley over the couscous and lightly toss. Serve the scallops immediately on a bed of couscous.

Justin Moore's Bbq Shrimp

Servings:2
Cooking Time: 10minutes

Ingredients:

- 1 pound peeled and deveined shrimp
- Cajun dry seasoning (I use Tony's)
- Good olive oil
- Fresh chopped garlic
- Freshly ground pepper
- Kosher salt

- Red pepper flakes

Directions:
1. Preheat the grill to 400°F using direct heat with a cast iron grate installed.
2. In a bowl, mix shrimp with all ingredients. Amounts of each depend on your taste … I like mine spicy, so I use a fair amount of Cajun spice and pepper flakes. Don't drown in olive oil, but make sure each shrimp is covered. Use skewers for cooking on the grill. Cook 3 to 4 minutes per side, then close all vents, and cook for 2 more minutes for a nice smoke flavor.
3. Serve over pasta, or as an appetizer with toasted French bread.

Grilled Rockefeller Oysters

Servings:12
Cooking Time: 5 Minutes

Ingredients:
- 12 shucked oysters
- 1/4 cup butter
- 1/2 cup red onions (chopped)
- 4 cloves garlic
- 1/2 cup Pinot Grigio
- 21/2 cups spinach (roughly chopped)
- 2 tbsp heavy cream
- 2 tbsp clam juice
- 1/2 cup mozzarella
- 2 tbsp crunchy bacon (chopped finely)

Directions:
1. Preheat the grill to 375°F using direct heat with a cast iron grate installed.
2. In a Stir-Fry and Paella Pan or other grill-safe pan, sauté onions in 2 tbsp butter on medium high until slightly translucent.

Add Pinot Grigio and simmer for 2 minutes. Add the rest of the butter and garlic and cook for 1 minute. Add spinach and cook until spinach is wilted, and then add the heavy cream and clam juice and cook for a few more seconds.
3. Top oysters with spinach mixture and mozzarella and place on a Perforated Cooking Grid or directly on the cooking grid for about 5 minutes or until the cheese bubbles. Sprinkle with bacon and enjoy!

Clam Bake

Servings: 6
Cooking Time: 30 Minutes

Ingredients:
- 2 lbs mussels, scrubbed and debearded
- 1 1/2 lbs kielbasa sausage, sliced into 1 inch chunks
- 1 1/2 lbs small potatoes (we like red potatoes)
- 2 large onions, roughly chopped
- 2 dozen littleneck clams, scrubbed
- 2 dozen steamer clams, scrubbed
- 2 cups dry white wine
- 2 Tablespoons olive oil
- 1 Tablespoon salt
- 1/2 Tablespoon black pepper

Directions:
1. Preheat the grill to 350°F using direct heat with a cast iron grate installed with the dutch oven on the grid.
2. Add olive oil and onion to the pot and cook until soft, about 5 minutes.
3. Add ingredients in layers in the following order: Kielbasa, Potatoes, Clams, Mussels.

4. Pour in the white wine and cover.

5. Lower the dome for 15-20 minutes or until the potatoes are cooked through and the shellfish have opened up.

6. Ladle out the sausage, potatoes, and seafood and strain the broth, taking care not to get any sand from the clams.

7. Serve on sheets of parchment paper with broth in small bowls for dipping and sipping.

8. If you have never tried parsnips before, they look like a white carrot and taste like a cross between a carrot and horseradish. When they are braised they become sweet, a perfect alternative to plain carrots.

Cedar Plank Salmon

Servings: 4
Cooking Time: 30 Minutes

Ingredients:

- 4 (4-6 oz each) salmon filets
- 2 cedar planks, soaked in water for 30 minutes
- 1/2 tsp salt
- 1/4 tsp black pepper
- 1/2 cup raspberry preserves
- 2 Tablespoons balsamic vinegar
- 1 jalapeño, chopped
- 1 clove garlic, minced

Directions:

1. Season salmon on both sides with salt and pepper.
2. Grilling:
3. Preheat the grill to 350°F using direct heat with a cast iron grate installed.

4. Place the plans on the grid and close the dome for 3 minutes.

5. Flip the planks and place the salmon on the heated side. Close the dome for 20 minutes.

6. Meanwhile, combine preserves, vinegar, jalapeño, and garlic in a small sauce pan and heat over low for 10 minutes, stirring occasionally.

7. Brush the salmon with the sauce and close the dome for another 5 minutes.

8. Serve with additional sauce.

Bobby Flay's Grilled Lobster Sandwiches

Servings:6
Cooking Time: 28 Minutes

Ingredients:

- 4 (2-pound) live lobsters
- 8 ears of corn
- Kosher salt and freshly ground black pepper
- Canola oil
- 1 serrano chile
- 3 ripe Hass avocados, peeled, pitted, and diced
- 1/4 cup creme fraiche
- 1/2 small red onion, finely diced
- 1/4 cup chopped fresh cilantro leaves
- Juice of 2 limes
- Few dashes of Tabasco sauce
- 6 soft sesame seed buns, split
- Fresh flat-leaf parsley, for garnish

Directions:

1. Bring a large pot of salted water to a boil. Working in batches, add the lobsters and boil for 10 to 12 minutes; they will be about

three-quarters done. Drain well and let cool. The lobsters can be parboiled a few hours in advance, covered, and kept refrigerated. Bring to room temperature before grilling.

2. Heat your grill to high for direct grilling.

3. Pull the outer husks down each ear of corn to the base. Strip away the silk from each ear of corn. Fold the husks back into place and tie the ends together with kitchen string. Place the ears of corn in a large bowl of cold water with 1 tablespoon salt for 10 minutes.

4. Remove the corn from the water and shake off the excess. Put the corn on the grill, close the cover, and grill, turning every 5 minutes, for 15 minutes, or until the kernels are almost tender when pierced with a paring knife.

5. Peel back the husks and remove. Brush the corn with oil and season with salt and pepper. Grill the ears until the kernels are lightly golden brown on all sides, about 5 minutes. Use a sharp knife to remove the kernels from the ears.

6. Brush the serrano with oil and grill, turning as needed, until charred all over, 6 to 8 minutes. Remove to a bowl, cover, and let sit for 10 minutes. Peel, seed, and roughly chop.

7. Put the avocados and crème fraîche in a medium bowl and mash slightly with a fork. Add the corn kernels, chile, diced red onion, cilantro, lime juice, Tabasco, and 2 tablespoons of oil. Season with salt and pepper and gently stir to combine.

8. Split each lobster down the underside with a heavy knife, taking care not to cut through the back shell, so that the lobster is still in one piece but the inside flesh is halved and exposed. Brush the cut sides of the lobsters with oil and season with salt and pepper. Grill the lobsters, cut side down, until lightly charred and heated through, 5 to 7 minutes.

9. Toast the buns, split side down, on the grill until lightly golden brown, about 20 seconds.

10. Remove the lobster meat from the shells and coarsely chop. Fill each bun with lobster, charred corn and avocado, and some parsley leaves.

Grilled Salmon

Servings:4
Cooking Time: 30 Minutes

Ingredients:

- Salmon fillets (with skin on), 4 to 5 ounces per serving
- 1/2 cup soy sauce
- 1/2 cup lemon juice
- 1/3 cup brown sugar, packed
- 1/4 cup vegetable oil
- 2 cloves garlic, crushed
- 2 tbsp butter, melted
- 2 tbsp maple syrup
- Your favorite commercial or homemade dry BBQ rub, to taste

Directions:

1. Combine soy sauce, lemon juice, brown sugar, oil and garlic and stir to dissolve sugar. Pour into a zippered-top plastic bag and add salmon. Marinate in the refrigerator for 3 to 6 hours.

2. After marinating, allow the salmon to stand at room temperature for 30 minutes before grilling, then pat dry with a paper towel.
3. Mix together the butter and maple syrup and brush over entire surface of the salmon. Sprinkle with a liberal amount of BBQ rub.
4. Preheat the grill to 350°F using direct heat with a cast iron grate installed, place the salmon on a fish grid and cook for 15 to 20 minutes. Salmon is done when a knife inserted in the fillet slides in easily with no resistance and flesh is no longer opaque.
5. Remove salmon; using a clean brush, brush on any remaining maple syrup/butter mixture and wrap in foil for 5 to 10 minutes before serving.

Grilled Mahi Mahi With Roasted Yellow Pepper Coulis

Servings:4
Cooking Time: 16 Minutes

Ingredients:

- 4 filets Mahi Mahi, 6 oz (170 g) each (or substitute any firm flesh fish such as grouper, wahoo or halibut)
- 1 tbsp (15 ml) extra virgin olive oil
- Salt and pepper
- 2 yellow peppers
- 1⁄4 cup + 1 tsp (65 ml) olive oil
- 1 tsp (5 ml) fresh lemon juice
- 1⁄2 tsp (3 ml) sugar
- Pinch of salt
- 1⁄4 cup (60 ml) heavy cream

Directions:

1. Season the fish with salt and pepper and marinate in one tablespoon olive oil for an hour.
2. Preheat the grill to 500°F using direct heat with a cast iron grate installed.
3. While the fish is marinating, prepare the coulis. Brush the yellow peppers with 1 teaspoon of olive oil. Place the peppers on the cooking grid and roast until soft, about 5-6 minutes, turning regularly until the skin is loose. Remove from the kamado grill and place in a container and seal for five to seven minutes. When the peppers are cool enough to handle, remove the stems, skins and seeds; reserve any juice that accumulated in the container or peppers.
4. Add peppers and juice, lemon juice, sugar, salt, cream and remaining olive oil in a blender and puree until smooth. Remove to a small pot and keep warm.
5. Grill the fish for 3 minutes or until nice grill marks have formed. Carefully turn the fish 90° to form nice cross hatch marks and cook 2 to 3 more minutes.
6. Flip the fish and finish cooking for 3 to 4 minutes; total cooking time should not exceed 8 minutes to ensure nice, moist fish.
7. Divide the sauce among four plates; top with the grilled fish. Serve with fried plantain and yellow rice and beans.

Spice-crusted Salmon With Rosé-glazed Vegetables

Servings:4
Cooking Time: 9minutes

Ingredients:

- 2 filets of salmon, skin off
- Classic Steakhouse Seasoning
- Hummus
- Kalamata olives
- Marinated artichokes
- Peppadew peppers, can substitute with roasted red bell peppers
- Roasted garlic
- ½ cup of rosé wine

Directions:

1. Preheat the grill to 400°F using direct heat with a cast iron grate installed, with a cast iron grate, flat sideup, and a cast iron skillet.
2. Liberally add the Classic Steakhouse Seasoning to the salmon and pat to adhere. Oil the cast iron grate, pat the salmon to get any access moisture off and place on the cast iron grate.
3. Remove from the grill. Serve the salmon over the hummus with the vegetables.
4. Add the roasted garlic and peppadew peppers to the cast iron skillet, cook for about 3-4 minutes.
5. Add the artichokes, olives and wine to the cast iron skillet. Flip the salmon and continue to cook for another 5 minutes

Maple-glazed Applewood Smoked Octopus

Servings:4
Cooking Time: 30 Minutes

Ingredients:

- Sushi grade, precooked, octopus tentacles
- 100% Canadian maple syrup

Directions:

1. Defrost the octopus and bring to room temperature.
2. Preheat the grill to 225°F using direct heat with a cast iron grate installed.
3. Place octopus tentacles on the indirect side of grill. Make sure your grid has been cleaned and seasoned with oil as to not tear the octopus while grilling.
4. After a few minutes, start to glaze the octopus tentacles with real 100% Canadian maple syrup. Continue to glaze every five minutes for the next half hour.
5. Remove the octopus from the grill and place onto a plate and open vents fully and open the lid of the kamado grill. Once the coals are red on the direct side, place the octopus on a clean oil-seasoned grill and glaze again.
6. After a minute or less, depending how it's cooking, you will want to flip and glaze the tentacles again. You don't want it so hot that the suction cups fall off, once they start to blacken it's time to flip them one last time with another glaze. Remove the tentacles to a platter and let rest for five minutes.
7. Slice tentacles into ½ inch thick pieces, drizzle one last time with maple syrup and serve. I prefer Kewpie Japanese Mayo, Kentucky Bourbon Barbecue Sauce or Hoison sauce for dipping.

Country Ham, Shrimp & Grits Kabobs

Servings:8
Cooking Time: 67 Minutes

Ingredients:

- 1 cup grits
- 1 cup shredded cheddar
- ¼ cup Oliver Farms Pecan Oil or Butter
- 1 cup country ham, fine dice
- ½ cup diced scallions
- ½ cup red pepper, fine dice
- ½ cup yellow pepper, fine dice
- 1 cup heavy cream
- 4 cups water
- 2 tsp salt
- ½ tsp black pepper
- ½ tsp dried thyme
- 1 pound 26-30 count shrimp, peeled and deveined, tail on
- ¼ cup olive oil
- 1 Tbsp Dijon mustard
- 1 tsp minced garlic
- 2 Tbsp fresh lemon juice
- Salt and pepper
- 1 red pepper, seeded, membrane removed, cut in 1" squares
- 1 yellow pepper, seeded, membrane removed, cut in 1" squares
- 1 red onion, peeled, cut in 1" squares, separate layers

Directions:

1. Cook diced ham in butter or oil until almost crisp. Add diced peppers and scallions. Cook until soft. Add cream, water and spices. Bring to a boil, gradually stir in grits. Bring back to a boil, then lower to simmer. Continue cooking for 45-60 minutes, adding a little more liquid if needed; they need to be thick. Remove from heat and stir in cheese until melted. Pour into greased 9" x 13" pan. Chill overnight.

2. Combine olive oil, Dijon, garlic, lemon juice, salt and pepper in a bowl. Add shrimp to mixture and marinate about 30 minutes

3. Cut grits into 1 square. Broil in oven on both sides until golden. Thread wooden skewers with 1 grits cube then pierce one piece each of red pepper, yellow pepper and red onion. Chill until ready to use.

4. Preheat the grill to 350°F using direct heat with a cast iron grate installed. Place skewers on the cooking grid; close dome and cook 5-7 minutes or until shrimp are opaque. Use spatula to carefully lift from underneath.

Grilled Swordfish With Corn-avocado Relish

Servings:2
Cooking Time: 2 Minutes

Ingredients:

- 1 1⁄2 pounds swordfish or any very fresh, white flesh fish, cut into 2 ounce pieces Olive oil
- Kosher salt
- Freshly ground black pepper
- 2 tablespoons olive oil
- 3 ears of corn, shucked
- 1 ripe beefsteak tomato, 1⁄4 inch diced
- 2 tablespoons fresh cilantro, chopped
- 1 Serrano pepper, stemmed, seeded, 1⁄4 inch diced Juice of 1 lime
- Sea salt
- 1 avocado

Directions:

1. Preheat the grill to 350°F using direct heat with a cast iron grate installed.

2. Add the olive oli and corn to a Stir-Fry &
Paella Pan or small sauté pan and cook for
about 2 minutes. Remove from the pan,
place in a medium bowl and allow to cool.
Combine the cooked corn, tomato, cilantro,
Serrano pepper, lime juice and a pinch of
sea salt. Peel and dice the avocado and mix
into the rest of the ingredients.

3. Toss the fish in a little oil, salt and pepper
and grill to your desired doneness. Top the
fish with the relish and serve immediately.

Grilled Tuna With Herb Butter

Servings:8
Cooking Time: 26minutes

Ingredients:

- 4 - 6 ounce tuna steaks
- 4 ounces herb butter (recipe follows)
- 4 bunches of Mixed Greens (Todd uses
cover crop harvested from the vineyard)
- 4 breakfast radishes, shaved
- Zest and juice of 2 lemons
- 2 tablespoons olive oil
- Flake salt
- Freshly cracked black pepper
- 4 ounces Rosé dressing (recipe follows)
- 2 oz. Italian flat leaf parsley, chopped
- 1 oz. Basil, chopped
- 1 oz. Mint, chopped
- Zest of one lemon
- ¼ cup green onions, minced
- 1 stick salted butter, room temperature
- 1 teaspoon freshly ground pepper
- 3 ounces Dry Rosé wine
- 1 teaspoon superfine sugar
- 1 clove garlic minced
- 1 ounce red wine vinegar
- ¼ teaspoon dried thyme

- ¼ teaspoon freshly ground black pepper
- ½ teaspoon salt
- 4 tablespoons extra virgin olive oil

Directions:

1. Preheat the grill to 650°F using direct heat
with a cast iron grate installed.

2. Season the fish with salt and pepper and grill
on each side for 2-3 minutes, rotating the
fish ¼ turn – halfway through the cooking
on each side – to achieve beautiful
cross-hatched grill lines. Once you have
given the fish a ¼ turn on the second side
put an ounce of the herb butter on each
piece of fish and finish cooking. Fish will
be a beautiful medium rare.

3. Meanwhile, in a small saucepan, combine
the smashed garlic, lemon zest, juice and
olive oil and heat on the grill.

4. To serve, arrange the washed cover crop on
four plates, drizzle with garlic lemon oil to
start the wilting process, sprinkle with sea
salt and cracked pepper. Place grilled fish
on top of salad. Garnish with shaved
radishes and a drizzle of the rosé
vinaigrette.

5. In a small bowl, combine all the ingredients
and mix well. Set butter aside till ready to
use.

6. Note: If you are making the butter a day in
advance, pull the butter out 20 minutes
before you grill the fish so it will soften
slightly. Will keep in the refrigerator for 4
days.

7. In a small bowl combine the ingredients
except for the oil. Once you have mixed the
ingredients together, slowly whisk in the
olive oil. Set dressing aside till ready to
serve. Mix again just before serving.

PORK

Croque Monsieur & Croque Madam

Servings: 6
Cooking Time: 30 Minutes

Ingredients:

- 4 slices smoked ham
- 4 slices sourdough bread
- 4 slices smoked provolone
- 1 cup shredded gruyere
- 2 tbsp butter
- 1 egg (for croque madam)
- 2 tbsp olive oil
- 1 cup béchamel sauce
- 1 tbsp butter
- 1 tbsp flour
- 3/4 cup warmed milk
- ¼ cup warmed heavy cream (added to milk to warm)
- 1 tsp salt (and salt to taste)
- 1 tsp course black pepper
- 2 tsp ground nutmeg

Directions:

1. Preheat the grill to 400°F using direct heat with a cast iron grate installed. Add the plancha griddle on half of the spander, with the half-moon baking stone, grid and a cast iron skillet on the other half.
2. To build the sandwiches, spread a layer of béchamel sauce on 2 slices of bread, then top with ham, provolone cheese, and the gruyere cheese; 2 slices for each piece of bread. Spread béchamel sauce on the last 2 slices of bread and place them on top of the sandwiches. On the top pieces of bread, spread more béchamel sauce and the remaining gruyere cheese on top.
3. Coat the plancha with olive oil and add both sandwiches. Cook until the bottom of the sandwich is golden brown and the provolone cheese is melted. Using your igniter, toast the top of the sandwich until it looks as if it has been broiled. Remove both sandwiches and set aside.
4. Melt butter on the plancha and fry your egg over easy or over medium. Top one sandwich with the egg; this is a Croque Madam, the sandwich without is a Croque Monsieur. Cut in half, and serve!
5. For the béchamel sauce, melt the butter in the cast iron skillet and add flour. Cook until the mixture turns golden brown and is fragrant. Slowly add the milk and cream while whisking the mixture to ensure there are no lumps. Once the milk and cream are completely mixed in removed the skillet from the heat and continue to whisk until the mixture has a creamy texture and is thick enough to cover the back of a spoon. If the mixture gets too thick, slowly mix in more milk until desired consistency. Add salt, pepper and nutmeg then set aside.

Brined Pork Roast

Servings: 2
Cooking Time: 45 Minutes

Ingredients:

- 1 gallon (3.8 L) of water

- 3 strips of thick bacon
- 8 oz (230 g) kosher salt
- 8 oz (230 g) dark brown sugar
- 1/4 cup (60 ml) whole black pepper
- 3 each whole cloves
- 2 cinnamon sticks
- 1 tsp (5 ml) ground nutmeg
- 6 sprigs thyme, or 1 tsp (5 ml) dry thyme
- 4 cloves of garlic, smashed with the side of a chefs knife

Directions:

1. In a large pot over medium heat, render bacon for 5 minutes. Add pepper, spices and garlic. Cook until fragrant. Add salt and brown sugar, cover with water and bring to a boil. Simmer until salt and brown sugar dissolve. Cool to room temperature then refrigerate overnight.
2. Only use the brine when it is very cold! Brine the meat under refrigeration for desired time and discard the brine when you remove the meat. Pat the meat dry and it is ready to use, no additional seasoning required!
3. Brining times Pork chops (1/2 in/13 mm) = 3 hours Pork chops (1 in/25 mm) = 4 hours Pork tenderloin = 3 hours Pork loin roast = 12 hours Boneless ham (5 lbs/2.6 kg) = 3 days
4. Preheat the grill to 450°F using direct heat with a cast iron grate installed.
5. Cook the pork until the internal temperature reaches 145°F, about 30-45 minutes. Remove to a platter, cover loosely with foil, and allow it to rest for 10 minutes.

Pork Belly Burnt Ends

Servings:2
Cooking Time: 180 Minutes

Ingredients:

- 1 pound piece of pork belly
- Your favorite barbecue rub
- Your favorite barbecue sauce
- Honey
- Apple juice

Directions:

1. Preheat the grill to 275°F using direct heat with a cast iron grate installed.
2. Trim the pork belly and cut the pork belly into 1" cubes. Cover the pork belly pieces in your favorite BBQ rub. Place pork belly pieces on the cooking grid and smoke for 3 hours, spraying with apple juice every hour until the pork reaches and internal temperature of 190°F.
3. Remove the pork pieces from the kamado grill and place them in an aluminum pan. Toss the pork belly pieces with BBQ sauce until evenly covered. Drizzle with honey and put the aluminum pan back on the grill. Cook the pork belly and cook for another hour until the sauce has reduced and caramelized.

Sriracha Pork Chops

Servings:4
Cooking Time: 9 Minutes

Ingredients:

- 4 (1") boneless pork chops
- 2 Tablespoons Better Than Bouillon Reduced Sodium Roasted Chicken Base

- 1 Tablespoon minced garlic
- 1 Tablespoon Sriracha sauce
- 1 Tablespoon freshly chopped cilantro
- 1 Tablespoon freshly squeezed lime juice
- ¼ cup brown sugar
- 2 teaspoons freshly minced ginger

Directions:

1. Instructions Mix the Roasted Chicken Base, garlic, sriracha, cilantro, lime juice, brown sugar and ginger in a small mixing bowl. Add half of the mixture to a resealable plastic bag and add the pork chops and refrigerate for at least 3 hours and up to 8 hours.
2. Reserve the rest of the marinade, covered and refrigerated until ready to use.
3. Preheat the grill to 425°F using direct heat with a cast iron grate installed.
4. Remove the pork chops from the marinade and place directly onto the grill. Grill for 4 minutes. Using tongs, turn the pork chops and brush with the reserved marinade. Grill for an additional 4 – 5 minutes.
5. Remove the pork chops from the kamado grill and brush with the reserved marinade before serving.
6. Serve immediately.

Apple-stuffed Pork Chops

Servings:12
Cooking Time: 50 Minutes

Ingredients:

- 6 (2-inch-thick) bone-in center-cut pork chops
- ½ tablespoon butter
- ¼ cup olive oil, divided

- ½ cup red onion, finely chopped
- ½ cup celery, finely chopped
- ½ cup Granny Smith apple, finely chopped
- 1½ cups herb stuffing mix
- 1½ cups chicken broth
- Ancho Chile & Coffee Seasoning

Directions:

1. Preheat the grill to 350°F using direct heat with a cast iron grate installed.
2. Melt the butter in a   Cast Iron Skillet. Add 1 tablespoon olive oil, onion, celery and apple; sauté 10 minutes or until vegetables are tender and the liquid evaporates. Add stuffing mix and broth; stir until liquid is absorbed; let stand 20 minutes.
3. Trim any excess fat from the pork chops and cut a slit in one side of each chop to form a pocket. Rub the pork chops evenly, inside and out, with olive oil and season liberally with the
4. Ancho Chile & Coffee Seasoning. Spoon stuffing mixture evenly into each pocket.
5. Raise the kamado grill temperature to 375°F. Place the pork chops on the cooking grid and roast for 30 to 40 minutes. Let stand 5 minutes before serving.

Porchetta

Servings: 16
Cooking Time: 270 Minutes

Ingredients:

- 1 boneless, skin-on pork belly, about 8lb (3.6kg) in total
- 4 tbsp kosher salt
- 4 tbsp rice flour

- 4lb (1.8kg) unpeeled red potatoes, diced large
- for the rub
- 2 tbsp kosher salt
- 2 tbsp ground black pepper
- 3 tbsp ground fennel seed
- 3 tbsp ground cumin
- 1 tbsp crushed red pepper flakes
- 3 tbsp chopped fresh thyme
- 12 garlic cloves, minced
- to smoke
- apple, hickory, or cherry wood chunks

Directions:

1. To make the rub, in a medium bowl, combine all the rub ingredients. Place pork belly skin side down on a large cutting board. Use your hands to rub the mixture deeply into the cracks and crevices of the belly meat (not the skin).

2. Roll pork belly into a tight log and set aside, seam side down. Using kitchen twine, cut lengths long enough to tie around pork and cut enough strings to space about 1 inch (5cm) apart. Lay them down along a cutting board, about 1 inch (2.5cm) apart each. Place the rolled pork seam side down on top of the strings. Working from the outermost strings toward the center, tie up pork tightly.

3. Combine salt and rice flour. Rub the flour mixture over the entire surface of porchetta. Wrap tightly with plastic wrap and refrigerate overnight or up to 3 days. Before smoking, remove from the fridge and let come to room temperature.

4. Preheat the grill to 300°F (149°C) using indirect heat with a standard grate installed.

Once hot, add the wood chunks, place pork in a V-rack, and set the rack in a drip pan. Place pork setup in the grill, close the lid, and roast until the internal temperature reaches 160°F, about 2 hours, basting with drippings every half hour.

5. After 1 hour of cooking, add potatoes to the drip pan and stir to coat. Continue roasting until a knife or skewer inserted into pork encounters very little resistance (aside from the outer layer of skin), about 2 more hours. Close the top and bottom vents to increase the temperature to 500°F (260°C) and continue roasting until the skin is completely crisp and potatoes are tender, about 20 to 30 minutes.

6. Remove pork from the grill and place on a cutting board tented with aluminum foil to rest for 15 minutes. Remove potatoes from drip pan and drain any excess fat. Season with salt and pepper to taste. Using a very sharp knife, slice the porchetta into disks about ¾ inch (2cm) thick. Serve with roasted potatoes.

Pineapple-glazed Kurobuta Bone-in Ham With Bourbon-cherry Sauce

Servings:8
Cooking Time: 188 Minutes

Ingredients:

- 1 Snake River Farms American Kurobuta Half Bone-In Ham
- 1 pineapple, cut into ¼ inch rounds, marinated in ¼ cup bourbon for 4 hours

(turn occasionally to keep the pineapple evenly coated)

- 2 cups pineapple juice
- ¼ cup bourbon
- 1 cup firmly packed dark brown sugar
- 1 tbsp cinnamon
- 1 tsp kosher salt
- 16 oz fresh cherries, pitted
- 1 cup pineapple juice
- ½ cup bourbon
- 2 tbsp unsalted butter
- 4 sprigs of thyme
- 1 tbsp balsamic glaze
- Salt to taste

Directions:

1. Preheat the grill to 325°F using direct heat with a cast iron grate installed.
2. Place the ham on the roasting rack and into the roasting pan. Place on the kamado grill and bake for 30 minutes. Glaze the ham with the pineapple glaze, reserving half. Bake for another 2 hours and coat with the remaining half of the glaze. Add the bourbon-soaked pineapple slices on top of the ham and secure with picks. Bake for another 30 minutes, or until the internal temperature is 155°F. Remove from the kamado grill and let rest for 10 minutes prior to slicing.
3. Remove the ham from the kamado grill and place on serving platter. Pour the leftover glaze from the roasting pan over the ham. Slice and serve the ham and top with the cherry sauce. Enjoy!
4. Preheat the grill to 325°F using direct heat with a cast iron grate installed.

5. In a small cast iron skillet, mix all of the ingredients for the glaze, place on the grid. Once the liquid starts to smoke, flambé the sauce using a long match (when you flambé, the bourbon flavor remains, the alcohol is removed, leaving most of the sugar behind). Continue cooking, stirring occasionally, until the liquid is reduced by half. Remove from the grill, carefully pour into a bowl and set aside.
6. 24-48 hours prior to cooking, soak the cherries in the bourbon in an airtight container, gently turning occasionally to keep the cherries evenly soaked.
7. In the dutch oven, mix all of the ingredients for the sauce, (including the bourbon the cherries soaked in). Place on the grid. Continue cooking until the liquid is reduced by half; this will take about as long as the ham is baking. Make sure to stir occasionally and add a small amount of water or pineapple juice if it thickens too quickly.

Pork Lettuce Wraps

Servings: 4
Cooking Time: 30 Minutes

Ingredients:

- 1⁄4 head of napa cabbage
- 2 carrots, peeled
- 1⁄2 head of broccoli, trimmed and cut into large pieces
- 11⁄2lb (680g) pork tenderloin, diced into small cubes
- 2 tbsp canola oil
- 1⁄2 cup water chestnuts, drained and thinly sliced

- 1 head of Bibb or iceberg lettuce, separated into leaves, to serve
- 1 bunch of scallions, sliced
- for the marinade
- 1/4 cup chopped fresh basil leaves
- 1/4 cup chopped fresh mint leaves
- 1/4 cup chopped fresh cilantro
- 1/4 cup thinly sliced fresh ginger
- 2 tbsp chopped garlic
- 1/2 cup canola oil
- 1/2 lime, cut into 8 pieces
- 2 tbsp kosher salt
- for the sauce
- 1/4 cup white wine
- 1/4 cup low-sodium soy sauce
- 2 tbsp hoisin sauce
- 1 tbsp rice wine vinegar
- 1 tbsp sugar
- 1 tbsp cornstarch
- 1 1/2 tsp chili garlic sauce

Directions:

1. To make the marinade, in a large bowl, combine all the marinade ingredients. Add pork to the marinade, and stir to coat. Cover with plastic wrap and refrigerate for at least 4 hours or overnight.
2. To make the sauce, in a small bowl, combine all the sauce ingredients. Set aside.
3. Preheat the grill to 425°F (218°C) using direct heat with a cast iron grate installed and a cast iron skillet on the grate. Arrange cabbage, carrots, and broccoli on the grate around the skillet. Close the lid and grill until beginning to soften and char, about 7 to 10 minutes. Remove the vegetables from the grill. Once cool enough to handle, finely shred the cabbage, julienne the carrots, and cut the broccoli into small pieces. Set aside.
4. Add oil to the skillet and heat until shimmering. Remove pork from the marinade and add to the skillet, discarding the marinade. Close the lid and grill until the meat is seared on all sides, about 3 to 5 minutes, stirring occasionally.
5. Add cabbage, carrots, broccoli, and water chestnuts to the skillet, close the lid, and cook for 2 to 3 minutes. Stir in the sauce, close the lid, and cook until the sauce has thickened, about 8 to 10 minutes.
6. Remove the skillet from the grill. To serve, scoop some of the pork and vegetable mixture into each lettuce leaf and top with scallions.

Pork Tenderloin Sliders

Servings: 12
Cooking Time: 20 Minutes

Ingredients:

- 3lb (1.4kg) pork tenderloin
- kosher salt and freshly ground black pepper
- 12 slider buns or rolls
- for the brine
- 1/2 cup kosher salt
- 1/2 cup packed light brown sugar
- 3 tbsp pickling spice
- 6 cups hot water
- for the glaze
- 12oz (340g) apple juice
- 1 cup bourbon
- 3 tbsp dark brown sugar
- 1 tbsp Dijon mustard
- 1/2 tsp kosher salt
- 1/2 tsp crushed red pepper flakes

- for the slaw
- 2 tbsp mayonnaise
- 2 tbsp whole grain mustard
- juice of 1 lemon
- 2 tbsp plain Greek yogurt
- 3 tbsp chopped fresh dill
- 1 fennel bulb, julienned
- 2 Granny Smith apples, julienned
- 1 red onion, thinly sliced into half-moons

Directions:

1. To make the brine, in a medium bowl, whisk together salt, brown sugar, pickling spice, and hot water until salt and sugar have dissolved. Add ice cubes a few at a time until the liquid is no longer hot. Pour the brine into a large resealable plastic bag, place pork tenderloin in the bag, and refrigerate for 2 to 4 hours. (Any extra brine can be refrigerated and saved for a later use.)

2. To make the slaw, in a large bowl, combine mayonnaise, mustard, lemon juice, Greek yogurt, and dill. Add fennel, apples, and onion. Season with salt and pepper to taste. Stir to combine, cover with plastic wrap, and refrigerate for 2 hours.

3. To make the glaze, in a medium saucepan, combine apple juice, bourbon, sugar, mustard, and salt. Bring to a boil on the stovetop over medium-high heat, then reduce heat to medium and simmer until the mixture has reduced to 1 cup, about 10 minutes, stirring occasionally. Stir in red pepper flakes, remove the saucepan from the heat, and refrigerate until needed.

4. Remove pork from the brine, pat dry with paper towels, place on a cutting board, and slice into medallions. Allow pork to come to room temperature, and season with salt and pepper to taste.

5. Preheat the grill to 400°F (204°C) using direct heat and a cast iron grate installed. Brush medallions on both sides with the glaze, place pork on grate, and close the lid. Cook for 3 to 5 minutes per side, brushing with glaze once or twice. Remove pork from the grill and serve topped with slaw on toasted slider buns.

Bourbon Grilled Pork Chops With Peach Barbecue Sauce

Servings:4
Cooking Time: 35 Minutes

Ingredients:
- 4 peaches (about 1¼ pounds), halved, pitted, and quartered
- 2 medium ripe tomatoes, seeded and quartered
- 1 tablespoon canola oil
- 1 sweet onion, chopped
- 1 tablespoon finely chopped fresh ginger
- ¼ cup apple cider vinegar
- ¼ cup honey
- 2 tablespoons bourbon
- ¼ cup coarse kosher salt, plus more for seasoning
- Freshly ground black pepper
- ¼ cup firmly packed brown sugar
- 2 cups boiling water
- 3 cups ice cubes
- 4 center cut, bone-in pork chops, about 1-inch thick, well trimmed (2¾ to 3 pounds)

Directions:

1. In the bowl of a food processor fitted with the metal blade, puree the peaches and tomatoes until smooth; set aside. Heat the oil in a medium saucepan over medium-high heat until shimmering. Add the onion and cook, stirring occasionally, until golden brown, 5 to 7 minutes. Add the ginger and cook, stirring frequently, until fragrant, 1 to 2 minutes. Add the reserved peach-tomato puree, vinegar, honey, and bourbon; season with salt and pepper. Bring the mixture to a boil over high heat, then decrease the heat to simmer. Cook until the mixture is reduced by half and thickened, about 20 minutes. Taste and adjust for the seasoning with salt and pepper. Reserve 1/4 cup sauce for basting the chops, and keep the remaining sauce warm in the saucepan until ready to serve.

2. Meanwhile, place the remaining 1/4 cup salt and brown sugar in a medium heatproof bowl. Pour over the 2 cups boiling water and stir to dissolve. Add the ice cubes and stir to cool. Add the pork chops, cover the bowl with plastic wrap, and refrigerate to marinate, about 30 minutes. (Do not marinate any longer or the pork will be too salty. If you can't cook it right at the 30-minute mark, remove the pork from the marinade and refrigerate until ready to continue.) Remove from the brine, rinse well, and thoroughly dry pat with paper towels. Set aside.

3. Season the pork chops with pepper. Preheat the grill to 400°F using direct heat with a cast iron grate installed. Place the pork chops on the cooking grid for 3 to 5 minutes per side or until the internal temperature reaches 145°F, brushing with Peach Barbecue Sauce in the last few minutes. Remove to a plate and cover with aluminum foil to rest and let the juices redistribute, 3 to 5 minutes. Serve immediately with reserved warm sauce on the side.

Double Smoked Maple Bourbon Glazed Ham

Servings:4
Cooking Time: 180 Minutes

Ingredients:

- 1 bone-in half spiral ham
- 3 cups apple juice
- 1 yellow onion, chopped
- 2 tbsp yellow mustard
- BBQ rub
- 1/2 cup pineapple juice
- 1/2 cup maple syrup
- 1 cup bourbon
- 1/4 tsp Dijon mustard
- 1 tsp cinnamon
- 1 cup brown sugar

Directions:

1. Preheat the grill to 275°F using direct heat with a cast iron grate installed.
2. Cover the ham in yellow mustard and add the BBQ rub. Put the apple juice and onion in a roasting pan then place the ham in a roasting rack in the roasting pan. Cook uncovered for 2 hours. Cover with foil and cook another hour. Uncover the ham, glaze, and cook for 30 minutes until the ham reaches an internal temperature of 140°.

3. Remove the ham from the kamado grill and let rest for 10 minutes. Slice and serve.
4. Add glaze ingredients to pan, bring to a boil, and reduce. Cook for 30 minutes or to your desired thickness.

Glazed Pork Belly With Sweet Potato

Servings:6
Cooking Time: 90 Minutes

Ingredients:

- 1¾ lbs (800 g) pork belly
- Agave nectar for drizzling
- Sea salt flakes
- 12 small sprigs of thyme
- 1 cup (240 ml) peach jam
- ½ cup (120 ml) barbecue sauce
- 3 tbsp (45 ml) bourbon whiskey
- 3 tbsp (45 ml) agave nectar
- 3 tbsp (45 ml) flower honey
- 6 tbsp (90 ml) smoked paprika powder (pimentón dulce)
- 2 tbsp (30 ml) dried thyme
- 1 tbsp (15 ml) garlic powder
- 1 tbsp (15 ml) onion powder
- 1 tbsp (15 ml) freshly ground black pepper
- 2 tbsp (30 ml) muscovado sugar or brown caster sugar
- 1 tbsp (15 ml) ground ginger
- pinch of chilli powder
- 6 sweet potatoes
- 7 tsp (35 ml) ground cinnamon
- 1 ⅓ cups (300 g) butter + extra for greasing the pan

Directions:

1. Preheat the grill to 375°F using direct heat with a cast iron grate installed.
2. Remove most of the fat layer from the pork belly, allowing a layer of ⅛inch (3-4 mm) of the soft white fat to remain. Cut the layer of fat on the pork belly crosswise.
3. Lightly rub the pork belly with the rub, reserving about ⅓ of the rub, and drizzle with agave nectar. Sprinkle with sea salt flakes and rub into the meat.
4. Sprinkle a handful Pecan Smoking Chips on the charcoal embers and add the platesetter for indirect cooking and Cast Iron Grid (flat side up). Lay the pork belly with the fat upwards on the grid and close the lid of the grill. Stabilize the temperature at 325°F and smoke the pork belly for 35-40 minutes.
5. With a basting brush, coat all sides of the pork belly with the glaze, reserving about of the glaze. Continue to cook until the internal temperature of the pork reaches 165°F. Remove from the kamado grill and loosely cover with foil. Raise the temperature of the kamado grill to 375°F.
6. Cut the pork belly into 1½inch (4 cm) cubes and lay them on the Cast Iron Plancha Griddle. Top with the remaining glaze and rub.
7. Place the Cast Iron Plancha Griddle with the pork on the grid. Grill for approximately 5 minutes until the glaze is caramelized and the pork is hot.
8. Put all ingredients for the glaze in a pan and bring to a boil on the stovetop while stirring often. Turn the heat to low and simmer gently for approximately 10 minutes.

9. Mix all ingredients for the rub together.

10. Wash and pat dry the sweet potatoes; cut into halves lengthwise. Grease a Cast Iron Skillet with butter and add the potatoes, cut edge upwards. Dust with 6 teaspoons of the cinnamon, cut 1 cup (225 g) of butter into thin slices and arrange the slices over the sweet potatoes.

11. Cover the skillet with foil and place in the grill; cook the potatoes for 45 minutes until the flesh is soft.

12. Scoop the cooked flesh of six potato halves and place in a bowl. Cut the remaining butter into cubes and add to the potatoes. Sprinkle with the remaining cinnamon and fold in gently. Scoop a sixth of the mixture onto each potato half. Garnish with the thyme and serve with the pork belly.

Reverse-seared Herb Crusted Bone-in Iberico Pork Loin

Servings:10
Cooking Time: 65 Minutes

Ingredients:
- 1 2.5-lb. bone-in pork loin
- 2 tbsp minced rosemary
- 2 tbsp minced oregano
- ¼ cup minced sage
- 2 tbsp minced thyme
- 6 cloves minced garlic
- 4 tbsp kosher salt
- 2 tbsp ground black pepper
- ½ cup Dijon mustard

Directions:
1. Set the kamado grill with the platesetter basket with one side indirect cooking (with the Half Moon Pizza & Baking Stone) and the other side preheat the grill to 300°F using direct heat with a cast iron grate installed.

2. Mix all ingredients for the crust in a bowl, and coat the pork loin with the crust. Place the roast on the indirect side of the kamado grill and roast for about 40 minutes. A good rule of thumb is to roast the pork for 20 minutes per pound. Once the internal temperature reaches 135°F move the pork loin to the direct side of the grill. Sear the pork for about 5 minutes per side or until the internal temperature is 145°F.

3. Let rest for 10 minutes, slice in between the bones and serve with your preferred sides.

Bacon Roses

Servings:12
Cooking Time: 10 Minutes

Ingredients:
- Bouquet of rose stems or wooden skewers
- 1 pack of bacon
- 40 toothpicks
- Sweet and Smoky Seasoning

Directions:
1. Preheat the grill to 350°F using direct heat with a cast iron grate installed.

2. Season the bacon with the Sweet and Smoky Seasoning. Take each slice of bacon and carefully roll it up.

3. Insert toothpicks in an X shape to the bottom of the bacon roll up.

4. Put bacon roll ups on kamado grill and allow them to cook until finished. Make sure the bacon isn't too crispy.

5. If using real flower stems, remove the flowers from the stems carefully. You may need to use scissors. Insert half a toothpick into the top of the stem. Remove the toothpicks from the bacon roll up and insert onto stem toothpick.

6. If using wooden skewers, simply remove the toothpicks from the bacon roll up and insert onto skewer.

7. Whichever method you choose, you will likely need to use a ribbon to tie the stems/skewers together towards the top so they don't fall over and put them in a vase or wrap.

Caribbean St. Louis Style Ribs

Servings: 6
Cooking Time: 300 Minutes

Ingredients:
- 2 racks (about 4 pounds) St. Louis Style Ribs
- 2 cups Chipotle Mango Lime Sauce
- 1 cup Habanero Rub
- 2 cups wood chips, soaked for 30 minutes in water
- 1/2 cup olive oil
- 1/4 cup lime juice

Directions:
1. Combine olive oil, lime juice, and Habanero Rub. Set aside.
2. Rinse the spare ribs under cold water and pat-dry with a paper towel.
3. Put them on a cutting board, bone side up.
4. Remove the membrane and the flap of meat running along the entire length of the ribs.

5. After trimming, generously apply rub, olive oil, and lime juice mixture.
6. Grilling:
7. Let it sit at room temperature while preheat the grill to 225°F using direct heat with a cast iron grate installed.
8. Add wood chips, put the plate setter in place, and place the grid on top.
9. Set the ribs on the grid, bone side down.
10. Close the dome and allow the ribs to smoke for 3 hours.
11. Brush the ribs with Chipotle Mango Lime Sauce and close the dome for another hour, or until the internal temperature reaches 185°F.
12. Once done, remove from the smoker and allow to cool for 15 minutes before carving.
13. Serve with more sauce on the side.

Smoked Andouille & Crawfish Gumbo

Servings: 12
Cooking Time: 180 Minutes

Ingredients:
- 1 green bell pepper, left whole
- 1 large yellow onion, halved
- 3 stalks of celery, left whole
- 1½ cups vegetable oil
- ½ cups all-purpose flour
- ½lb (225g) andouille sausage
- 1lb (450g) smoked sausage
- 8 cups chicken stock
- 1lb (450g) crawfish meat
- 1½ tsp kosher salt
- ½ tsp ground cayenne pepper (optional)
- 2 tbsp chopped fresh flat-leaf parsley

- 2 tbsp sliced scallions
- 6 cups cooked white rice, to serve (optional)

Directions:

1. Preheat the grill to 325°F (163°C) using direct heat with a cast iron grate installed and a dutch oven on the grate. Place pepper, onion, and celery on the grate around the dutch oven, close the grill lid, and grill until beginning to soften and char, about 6 to 8 minutes. Transfer the vegetables to a cutting board. Seed and dice the pepper, and dice the celery and onion. Set aside.

2. In the hot dutch oven, heat oil until shimmering. Add flour and stir. Close the grill lid and cook for 20 to 25 minutes, stirring every 5 minutes. While the roux cooks, place the sausages on the grate next to the dutch oven, close the grill lid, and grill until slightly charred, about 10 minutes. Remove the sausages from the grill, finely dice andouille and slice smoked sausage into bite-sized pieces.

3. Once the roux looks dark brown in color, add sausages, peppers, onions, and celery to the dutch oven, and stir to coat. Close the grill lid and cook until the vegetables are soft, about 8 to 10 minutes.

4. Add stock to the dutch oven, and stir until the roux and stock are well combined. Leaving the dutch oven uncovered, close the grill lid and reduce the heat by closing the top and bottom vents most of the way. Cook for 90 minutes, stirring occasionally. Add crawfish to the dutch oven, close the grill lid, and cook for 15 minutes more.

5. Remove the dutch oven from the grill and let sit for 5 minutes before skimming any fat that has risen to the surface. Stir in salt and cayenne (if using). Taste and adjust the seasonings as needed. Stir in parsley and scallions, and serve immediately with white rice (if using).

Bone-in Loin Roast

Servings: 8
Cooking Time: 120 Minutes

Ingredients:

- 1 5-pound bone-in pork loin roast
- 1/2 cup olive oil
- 1/3 cup fresh rosemary
- 1/3 cup fresh thyme
- 2 tsp salt
- 1 tsp black pepper
- 6 cloves garlic, minced
- 4 lemons, juiced and zested

Directions:

1. Remove the pork loin from the fridge, rinse, and pat dry.
2. In a food processor, combine olive oil, herbs, lemon juice and zest, and garlic and pulse to combine into a paste.
3. Slather the pork loin on all sides with the oil and herb mixture and set aside for 30 minutes.
4. Grilling:
5. Preheat the grill to 400°F using direct heat with a cast iron grate installed.
6. Place the roast on the grid and close the dome for 1 1/2 hour. The roast is done when a thermometer inserted into the center of the meat reaches 150°F.
7. Remove the roast and allow it to rest for 20 minutes before carving.

Prosciutto Wrapped Cheese Dogs

Servings:6
Cooking Time: 12 Minutes

Ingredients:

- 6 Nature's Own 100% Whole Wheat Hot Dog Rolls
- 1 teaspoon Italian seasoning
- 3 pieces string cheese
- 6 prosciutto slices
- 2 teaspoons olive oil
- 6 fat-free hot dogs
- Dijon mustard
- Chopped tomato

Directions:

1. Preheat the grill to 375°F using direct heat with a cast iron grate installed.
2. Cut a lengthwise slit down center of each hot dog; do not cut all the way through bottom or ends. Sprinkle Italian seasoning evenly over hot dogs, rolling to coat.
3. Pull each string cheese piece in half vertically, forming 6 pieces. Stuff 1 cheese piece into each hot dog slit. Wrap 1 prosciutto slice around each stuffed hot dog, encasing completely. Brush prosciutto lightly with oil. Place hot dogs on baking sheet.
4. Cook 10 to 12 minutes or until heated through and cheese melts. Place hot dogs in rolls. Top with mustard, tomato and basil.

Grilled Chicken Breasts

Servings: 4
Cooking Time: 15 Minutes

Ingredients:

- 4 skinless, boneless chicken breasts, about 1½lb (680g) in total
- kosher salt and freshly ground black pepper
- 2 nectarines, halved and pitted
- 1 jalapeño pepper, seeded and minced
- 2 cups blackberries, roughly chopped
- 4 tbsp chopped fresh cilantro
- 2 tbsp balsamic vinegar, plus more to taste
- for the brine
- ¼ cup kosher salt
- ¼ cup packed light brown sugar
- 2 tbsp pickling spice
- 3 cups hot water

Directions:

1. To make the brine, in a medium bowl, whisk together all the brine ingredients until salt and sugar have dissolved. Add ice cubes a few at a time until the liquid is no longer hot. Place chicken in a resealable plastic bag and add the brine to cover. (Any extra brine can be refrigerated and saved for a later use.) Refrigerate for 30 minutes.
2. Remove chicken from the brine, pat dry with paper towels, and season with salt and pepper to taste. Set aside and allow to come to room temperature.
3. Preheat the grill to 350°F (177°C) using direct heat with a cast iron grate installed. Place nectarines on the grate skin side up, close the lid, and grill until softened and slightly charred, about 2 minutes. Remove from the grill and dice.
4. In a medium bowl, combine nectarines, jalapeño, blackberries, and cilantro. Add vinegar and toss to combine, adding more vinegar (if desired).

5. Spoon some of the liquid from the salsa over the chicken breasts and rub into the meat. Place chicken on the grate, close the lid, and grill until the meat reaches an internal temperature of 160°F (71°C), about 4 to 6 minutes per side. Remove chicken from the grill and top with the blackberry salsa before serving.

Ham & Cheese Panini

Servings:4
Cooking Time: 10 Minutes

Ingredients:
- 8 slices Natures Own 100% whole wheat bread
- ¼ cup spicy brown mustard
- 8 slices sharp white Cheddar cheese
- 2 cups packed baby arugula
- 1 ripe Bartlett pear, cut into 20 thin slices
- ½ pound deli-sliced smoked ham
- Olive Oil

Directions:
1. Preheat the grill to 400°F using direct heat with a cast iron grate installed.
2. Spread mustard evenly over 1 side of each bread slice. Top each of 4 bread slices with 1 slice cheese and half the arugula. Add the pear and ham slices; top with remaining arugula, cheese and bread slices.
3. Press sandwiches together slightly, brush outside of sandwiches lightly with oil Cook sandwiches on the griddle, turning once, until browned and cheese melts.

Injected Pork Shoulder

Servings:12

Cooking Time: 480 Minutes

Ingredients:
- One 7 to 8 pound pork butt, fat cap trimmed off
- Tony Chachere's Injectables Roasted Garlic & Herb Marinade
- Tony Chachere's Spice N' Herbs Seasoning
- Tony Chachere's Original Creole Seasoning
- Olive oil

Directions:
1. Preheat the grill to 275°F using direct heat with a cast iron grate installed.
2. Inject the pork shoulder with the marinade. Rub the meat with the oil and then sprinkle liberally with the seasonings.
3. Put the butt in the kamado grill and cook until the internal temperature is 195°F; this should take 8 to 10 hours.
4. Using meat claws, transfer the meat to a big pan; it will be very tender. Shred the meat, discarding the fat and bones; it should just fall apart. Serve on fluffy white buns topped with barbecue sauce and cole slaw.

Dr. Bbq's All Aces Baby Back Ribs

Servings:9
Cooking Time: 60 Minutes

Ingredients:
- 3 slabs pork loin back ribs, about 6 pounds total
- 1 cup apple juice
- 1 cup KC Style Sweet & Smoky Barbeque Sauce

- 1 cup Vidalia Onion Sriracha Barbeque Sauce
- 1/4 cup raw sugar
- 3 tablespoons kosher salt
- 3 tablespoons paprika
- 2 tablespoons chili powder
- 1 teaspoon granulated onion
- 1 teaspoon granulated garlic
- 1 teaspoon cayenne

Directions:

1. Preheat the grill to 300°F using direct heat with a cast iron grate installed. Peel the membrane off the back of the ribs. Season the ribs liberally on all sides with Ray's Rub. Let the ribs rest for 10 minutes so the rub will get tacky, then place in a rib rack and cook for two hours.

2. Lay out three double sheets of heavy duty aluminum foil. Place a slab on each meaty side up. Fold up the edges and add 1/3 cup of apple juice to each packet. Put the ribs back on the kamado grill and cook for 1 hour or until tender when poked with a toothpick.

3. When the ribs are tender to your liking, remove from foil and return to kamado grill meaty side down. Combine the two sauces and mop/brush the ribs with a liberal coating. Cook for 15 minutes. Flip the ribs and brush the top of the ribs with sauce. Cook for 15 minutes. Brush with a second coat of sauce. Cook for 30 minutes until the sauce is set. Remove to a cutting board and cut each slab into 3 even pieces.

4. Add all ingredients in a bowl and mix.

Grilled Italian Sausage & Orzo Soup

Servings: 4
Cooking Time: 35 Minutes

Ingredients:

- 2 Italian sausages (Shannon uses Beyond Meat hot Italian sausages)
- 1 bell pepper (Shannon uses half yellow and half red), quartered, membrane and seeds removed
- 1 small to medium onion, peeled and quartered
- 1 15-oz can diced tomatoes with Italian seasoning
- 3 cups vegetable broth
- 1 medium zucchini, diced or two big handfuls of spinach
- ½ cup orzo, uncooked
- 1 tbsp Italian seasoning
- 3 cloves of garlic, minced
- Salt and pepper to taste
- Suggested toppings: fresh grated parmesan cheese and/or pearl mozzarella balls

Directions:

1. Preheat the grill to 375°F using direct heat with a cast iron grate installed.

2. Add the sausages, onions and peppers to the grid and grill until softening and charred. Dice into bite size pieces.

3. Lower the temperature of the kamado grill to 325°F with the dutch oven in the kamado grill to preheat.

4. Add all of the ingredients into the dutch oven and simmer for about 35 minutes or until the orzo is cooked, stirring every

10-12 minutes. Add more water as needed or to make the soup thinner if desired.

5. Serve with fresh grated parmesan cheese and/or pearl mozzarella balls.

Beer Brined Loin Chops

Servings: 6
Cooking Time: 15 Minutes

Ingredients:

- 6 boneless pork loin chops, cut 1 to 1 1/4 inch thick
- 2 cups water
- 2 cups ice
- 1/4 cup coarse salt
- 2 Tablespoons brown sugar
- 6 cloves garlic, minced
- 1 (12 oz) beer (we like Samuel Adams Cherry Wheat for its sweet and tart fruity flavor)

Directions:

1. In a small sauce pan, heat water, salt, and sugar together until salt and sugar are dissolved. Add cold beer, garlic, and ice.
2. Submerge pork chops into brine and allow to sit in the refrigerator for at least 2 hours and as long as overnight.
3. Remove the chops from the fridge and brine and pat dry.
4. Grilling:
5. Preheat the grill to 425°F using direct heat with a cast iron grate installed.
6. Place the pork chops on the grid and close the dome for 5 minutes.
7. Flip the pork chops and close the dome for another 5 minutes.

8. Close all vents and allow the pork to sit for another 3-5 minutes or until the internal temperature reaches 150°F.

Pork Cacciatore

Servings:4
Cooking Time: 122 Minutes

Ingredients:

- 6 pounds boneless pork shoulder
- 1 1⁄4 teaspoon sea salt
- 3⁄4 teaspoon freshly ground pepper
- 2 tablespoons olive oil
- 1 large red bell pepper, sliced
- 1 large green bell pepper, sliced
- 2 yellow onions, sliced
- 3-4 cloves garlic, chopped
- 2 teaspoons dried basil
- 2 teaspoons dried parsley
- 1 teaspoon dried thyme
- 1 teaspoon red pepper flakes, optional
- 1 cup low sodium chicken broth
- 1 28 ounce can petite diced tomatoes
- 3 tablespoons tomato paste

Directions:

1. Preheat the grill to 350°F using direct heat with a cast iron grate installed.
2. Take pork shoulder out of package and wipe down with a paper towel. Season with salt and pepper.
3. Heat your dutch oven in the grill. Add in oil and let it get nice and hot. Add in pork and sear all sides for about 2 minutes; you want to create a nice sear. Add in peppers, onions and garlic. Cook for about 5 minutes stirring around using a wooden spoon.

4. Add in basil, parsley, thyme and red pepper flakes. Pour in chicken broth and diced tomatoes. Stir to incorporate all of the ingredients. Add in tomato paste and press against the pan with the back of your spoon to help incorporate into the liquid. Cover and let cook 2 hours.

5. Remove from grill. Use a large spoon and skim off the fat then go ahead and pull apart the pork or serve in large chunks with the peppers and onions. Enjoy!

Mona Lisa's Glazed Smoked Ham

Servings:4
Cooking Time: 270 Minutes

Ingredients:
- 1 Ham 10-12 lbs
- 1-20 oz. can round sliced pineapple
- 1 jar maraschino cherries
- 2 boxes brown sugar

Directions:
1. Preheat the grill to 350°F using direct heat with a cast iron grate installed..
2. Rinse ham with cold water, pat dry, and set aside.
3. Take the juice from the pineapple and mix well with the brown sugar to make a nice thick syrupy glaze. Next add the pineapple to the ham putting a cherry in the hole of each pineapple round. Finally pour the glaze over the ham.
4. Loosely cover the ham with aluminum foil and cook for 3-4 hours basting the ham with the pan juice every 30 min.
5. Let stand for 30 min. Slice and serve.

Braised Carnitas With Chimichurri Sauce

Servings:8
Cooking Time: 300 Minutes

Ingredients:
- 4 lbs. boneless pork shoulder
- 3 tbsp olive oil
- 1 can of Coca-Cola
- 2 oranges, juiced
- 6 limes, 2 juiced and 4 sliced in wedges for serving
- 2 jalapeños, seeded and chopped
- 1 yellow onion, diced
- 2 tbsp garlic, minced
- Flour tortillas
- 2 tbsp oregano
- 3 tsp cumin
- 3 tbsp olive oil
- 3 tbsp salt
- 3 tbsp pepper
- 3 tsp. minced garlic
- ½ tbsp. salt (more to taste if needed)
- 2 cups cilantro, finely chopped
- 3 tbsp oregano
- 1 cup parsley, finely chopped
- ¼ cup minced red onion
- 1 lime, juiced
- 2 tbsp. white wine vinegar
- 1 cup EVOO

Directions:
1. Preheat the grill to 400°F using direct heat with a cast iron grate installed.
2. Rinse pork and pat dry. Season the entire pork shoulder liberally with the rub.

3. Place a dutch oven on the grid and add the oil to heat. Add the pork shoulder and sear on all sides until lightly browned.

4. Remove the dutch oven from the grill. Add the platesetter for indirect cooking and stabilize the kamado grill at 300°F.

5. Arrange the shoulder in the dutch oven with the fat cap facing up. Pour the Coca-Cola, orange juice and lime juice into the dutch oven. Add the jalapeños, onion and garlic over the top of the pork. Cook for 4 ½ to 5 hours until meat pulls apart easily.

6. Mix all the ingredients together.

7. Crush the garlic and salt together to make a paste. Add cilantro, oregano, parsley, red onion and lime juice until combined. Add white wine vinegar and EVOO, mix and add salt/pepper to taste. Serve over the carnitas with tortillas.

Roasted Ham With Coca-cola Mustard Glaze

Servings:12
Cooking Time: 120 Minutes

Ingredients:
- 6-8 pound smoked ham
- 4 cups Coca-Cola
- 2 tbsp mustard (spicy brown, yellow or Dijon)

Directions:
1. Preheat the grill to 300°F using direct heat with a cast iron grate installed.
2. Place ham in a Disposable Drip Pan, an aluminum foil pan or a metal pan lined with foil. Score the top with a sharp knife, making shallow cuts about an inch apart,

then repeat in the opposite direction making a crisscross pattern. Place in the kamado grill and cook for about 1 hour.

3. While the ham is cooking the first hour, reduce the Coca-Cola and mustard in a saucepan over medium heat until reduced to 1 cup.

4. After 1 hour, baste the ham liberally with the glaze. Repeat glazing about every 10 minutes, using drippings in the pan as well. Cook an additional 45 – 60 minutes or until nicely glazed. Let rest 10 minutes before slicing.

Bacon-wrapped Scotch Eggs

Servings: 8
Cooking Time: 30 Minutes

Ingredients:
- 8 large eggs
- 1lb (450g) pork sausage, casings removed
- 16 bacon strips
- for the sauce
- 1 cup mayonnaise
- 1 cup coarse ground mustard
- kosher salt and freshly ground black pepper

Directions:
1. On the stovetop over high heat, bring a large pot of water to a boil. Once boiling, add eggs and boil for 4 minutes. Carefully drain, then transfer eggs to an ice bath to chill for 30 minutes. Peel and set aside.
2. To make the sauce, in a small bowl, combine mayonnaise and mustard, and season with salt and pepper to taste. Refrigerate until ready to serve.

3. Preheat the grill to 475°F (246°C) using indirect heat with a standard grate installed. Divide the sausage into 8 equal portions. Form one portion of sausage meat into a thin, flat patty and gently wrap it around one egg, making sure the egg is fully enclosed in an even layer of meat. Repeat with the remaining sausage and eggs, then wrap each egg with 2 bacon strips, completely covering the sausage with bacon.

4. Place eggs directly on the grate, close the lid, and cook until the sausage is cooked through and the bacon is crisp, about 20 minutes. Rotate the eggs a few times while cooking to ensure the bacon gets crispy.

5. Remove eggs from the grill, cut them in half, and arrange on a serving dish. Serve immediately with the sauce.

Chinese St. Louis Style Ribs

Servings: 6
Cooking Time: 240 Minutes

Ingredients:
- 2 racks St. Louis Style Ribs
- 2 cups Chinese Barbecue Sauce (Char Sui)
- 1 cup Asian Rub
- 2 cups wood chips, soaked for 30 minutes
- 1/4 cup olive oil

Directions:
1. Rinse the spare ribs under cold water and pat-dry with a paper towel.
2. Put them on a cutting board, bone side up.
3. Remove the membrane along the entire length of the ribs.

4. After trimming, generously brush with olive oil and apply the rub.
5. Grilling:
6. Let it sit at room temperature while preheat the grill to 225°F using direct heat with a cast iron grate installed.
7. Add wood chips, put the plate setter in place, and place the grid on top.
8. Set the ribs on the grid, bone side down.
9. Close the dome and allow the ribs to smoke for 3 hours.
10. Brush the ribs with Chinese Barbecue Sauce and close the dome for another hour, or until the internal temperature reaches 185°F.
11. Once done, remove from the smoker and allow to cool for 15 minutes before carving.
12. Serve with more sauce on the side.

Apple Cinnamon Pork Chops

Servings: 4
Cooking Time: 20 Minutes

Ingredients:
- 4 bone-in ribeye (rib) pork chops, about ¾ inch thick
- Salt and pepper
- 3 tablespoons butter, divided
- 2 apples, peeled, cored and thinly sliced
- 1 large white onion, halved and thinly sliced
- 2 tablespoons brown sugar, packed
- 2 teaspoons cinnamon
- Pinch cayenne
- ⅔ cup apple cider
- ⅓ cup heavy cream

Directions:

1. Preheat the grill to 400°F using direct heat with a cast iron grate installed.

2. Generously season the chops with salt and pepper on both sides. Set aside.

3. In the Half Moon Cast Iron Griddle melt 2 tablespoons of butter. Immediately add the pork chops and cook until brown, about 3 minutes per side. Transfer to a plate and set aside.

4. In the Half Moon Cast Iron Griddle, still at 400°F, melt 1 tablespoon of butter. Immediately add the apples and onion and let them cook, until the onion is translucent, about 5 minutes. Stir in the brown sugar, cinnamon and cayenne. Next, stir in the apple cider and cream. Then add the pork chops, nestling them into the liquid, and cook until the internal temperature of the pork reaches between 145°F. for medium rare and 160°F for medium. It should take about 3-4 minutes per side.

5. Serve the chops with the apple mixture spooned on top.

Bacon-wrapped Pork Tenderloin

Servings:8
Cooking Time: 50 Minutes

Ingredients:
- 2 whole pork tenderloins, silver skin removed
- 16 slices of bacon
- Ancho Chili & Coffee Seasoning
- Extra virgin olive oil

Directions:
1. Preheat the grill to 350°F using direct heat with a cast iron grate installed.

2. Coat the tenderloins with extra virgin olive oil and season with Ancho Chili & Coffee Seasoning to your liking. Wrap each tenderloin in 8 slices of bacon, putting the bacon under the tenderloin and wrapping upwards so the ends of the bacon are on top.

3. Place the pork on the indirect side of the kamado grill and cook for 45-50 minutes or until the internal temperature reaches at least 145°F. Transfer the tenderloins to the direct side of the kamado grill and sear on each side until bacon is crispy. Slice and enjoy!

Gyro Brat Hoagie

Servings:6
Cooking Time: 15 Minutes

Ingredients:
- 1 package (19 ounces) Johnsonville Original Bratwurst
- 1 loaf (1 pound) French bread
- 1 small onion, thinly sliced
- 1 medium tomato, thinly sliced
- 8 ounces sour cream
- 1/2 medium cucumber, peeled, seeded and finely chopped
- 2 cloves garlic, minced
- 2 teaspoon fresh parsley, chopped
- 1/4 teaspoon salt
- 1/4 teaspoon cracked black pepper, optional

Directions:
1. Preheat the grill to 350°F using direct heat with a cast iron grate installed.

2. Grill brats according to package directions. When cool enough to handle, cut into 1/4 inch bias slices.

3. Slice French bread lengthwise and transfer to a Perforated Cooking Grid. Arrange brat slices on bread bottom.

4. Cook on kamado grill until bread is lightly browned. Remove from grill. Top with the sauce, onion and tomato.

5. In a bowl, combine sauce ingredients. Cover and refrigerate until serving.

Center Cut Pork Loin Chops With Pineapple Salsa

Servings: 6
Cooking Time: 22 Minutes

Ingredients:

- 6 center cut, bone in pork loin chops cut 1 to 1 1/4 inch thick
- 3 cups water
- 2 cups ice
- 1 cup apple juice
- 1/4 cup Kosher salt
- 1 Tablespoon whole peppercorns
- 4 cloves garlic, smashed
- 2 cups pineapple, diced into 1/4 inch cubes
- 1/2 cup red onion, finely diced
- 2 Tablespoons lime juice
- 1 jalapeño, finely diced
- 1/4 tsp salt

Directions:

1. In a small saucepan, heat water and salt until the salt dissolves. Add apple juice, ice, garlic, and peppercorns.

2. Submerge the pork chops for a minimum of 1 hour or up to overnight in the fridge.

3. Remove the pork chops from the brine and pat dry.

4. Grilling:

5. Preheat the grill to 425°F using direct heat with a cast iron grate installed.

6. Place the pork chops on the grid and close the dome for 10 minutes.

7. Meanwhile, combine salsa ingredients and set aside.

8. Turn pork chops and close the dome for an additional 10-12 minutes or until the internal temperature near the bone reaches 150°F.

9. Remove the chops and top with the salsa.

Dizzy Pig Pork Shoulder

Servings:12
Cooking Time: 660 Minutes

Ingredients:

- 7.5-10 lb pork butt (also called pork shoulder blade roast, Boston butt)
- 1/3 cup of Dizzy Pig Seasoning
- Salt
- 2 or 3 chunks of smoking wood (hickory is a natural on pork)
- 1/2 cup of peach nectar
- Hot sauce (optional, and to taste mixed in with peach nectar)

Directions:

1. Trim excess fat and silver skin. Leave fat cap on one side. Shake a light layer of coarse salt onto all sides of the pork butt.

2. Cover generously with Dizzy Pig Seasoning and press in with hands to adhere. Let rub melt in for 20 minutes or more while you prepare grill.

3. Prepare fire in grill, starting with a small amount of charcoal in the firebox. Once all charcoal is burning and kamado grill has warmed up to 300°F or more, lay wood chunks on coals, and cover with more charcoal to fill firebox.

4. Add the platesetter with legs up and drip pan or foil to catch drippings. Place cooking grid on platesetter legs.

5. Stabilize kamado grill at 250°F, and wait 20 minutes or more until smoke is thin with a light smoky aroma. Place seasoned pork butt on grid, fat cap down. Cook for approximately 8 hours, or until outside crust (bark) is caramelized and firm.

6. After 8 hours, or when the meat reaches 170°F internal temperature, double wrap the butt in heavy-duty aluminum foil. Before sealing foil, pour in peach nectar/hot sauce mixture. For a little extra layer of flavor, grind a couple teaspoons of Dizzy Pig Seasoning finely and add to liquid.

7. Return to kamado grill and cook until 200°F internal temperature in the center. Remove from grill, cover with towels, a blanket or place in cooler to rest for at least 1 hour and up to 3.

8. Pull, shred, chop or chunk to your preference. Add salt, fine ground rub to taste. Enjoy!

Honey Chipotle Grilled Wings

Servings: 6
Cooking Time: 25 Minutes

Ingredients:

- 3lb (1.4kg) chicken wings (about 18 wings), cut into sections
- 1 tbsp kosher salt
- 1 tbsp ground black pepper
- 1 tbsp chili powder
- 1/2 cup rice flour
- 1 tbsp chopped fresh cilantro, to garnish
- for the brine
- 1/3 cup kosher salt
- 1/3 cup packed light brown sugar
- 2 tbsp pickling spice
- 4 cups hot water
- for the glaze
- 3 chipotle peppers in adobo
- 1 tbsp adobo sauce
- 1/2 cup honey
- 2 tbsp fresh lemon juice
- 2 tbsp soy sauce

Directions:

1. To make the brine, in a medium bowl, whisk together salt, brown sugar, pickling spice, and water until salt and sugar have dissolved. Add ice cubes a few at a time until the liquid is no longer hot. Place chicken pieces into two resealable plastic bags and add brine to cover. (Any extra brine can be refrigerated and saved for a later use.) Refrigerate for 30 minutes.

2. In a large bowl, combine salt, pepper, chili powder, and rice flour. Working with a small amount of chicken at a time, dredge the meat, shaking off any excess flour. Arrange wings in a single layer on a wire rack placed over a baking pan. Refrigerate uncovered for 8 hours.

3. To make the glaze, combine peppers, honey, lemon juice, and soy sauce in a blender or

food processor and purée until smooth. Transfer glaze to a small bowl.

4. Preheat the grill to 375°F (191°C) using direct heat with a cast iron grate installed. Remove chicken from the brine and pat dry with paper towels. Place wings skin side down on the grate, close the lid, and grill until the skin begins to brown and crisp, about 8 to 12 minutes per side. In the final 5 minutes of cooking, brush the glaze all over wings.

5. Transfer wings to a serving dish, coat with more glaze, sprinkle with cilantro, and serve immediately.

Smoked Spicy Korean Spare Ribs

Servings:12
Cooking Time: 300 Minutes

Ingredients:

- 2 racks pork spareribs, membranes removed
- Sweet and Smoky Seasoning
- 1 green onion, sliced
- 1 red jalapeño pepper, sliced
- ½ cup gochujang
- ¼ cup hoisin sauce
- ¼ cup ketchup
- ¼ cup honey
- ¼ cup soy sauce
- ¼ cup Korean rice wine
- 1 tbsp unseasoned rice vinegar
- 2" piece fresh ginger, finely gated
- 3 cloves of finely grated garlic
- 1 tbsp ground white pepper

Directions:

1. Preheat the grill to 250°F using direct heat with a cast iron grate installed.

2. Trim the excess fat from the ribs and cover in the Sweet and Smoky Seasoning.

3. Put in the ribs bone side down in the grill. After cooking for 3 hours glaze with Korean BBQ sauce. Cook for another hour.

4. Raise the temperature to 300° and glaze the ribs with the Korean BBQ sauce. Place back in the kamado grill for an hour.

5. When the meat pulls from the bone it is time to remove from the grill. Garnish with the green onion and jalapeño pepper. Enjoy!

6. Mix all the Korean BBQ ingredients together and set in the refrigerator.

Seared Duck

Servings: 8
Cooking Time: 20

Ingredients:

- 2lb (1kg) skin-on duck breasts
- ¼ cup scallions, thinly sliced, to garnish
- for the marinade
- 1 cup huckleberries, fresh or frozen
- 1 bunch of scallions, thinly sliced
- ½ bunch of fresh cilantro
- 2 garlic cloves, chopped
- 1 tsp finely grated lime zest
- 1 tsp finely grated orange zest
- ¼ cup fresh lime juice
- ¼ cup fresh orange juice
- ¼ cup low-sodium soy sauce
- 2 tbsp vegetable oil
- 2 tbsp kosher salt

Directions:

1. To make the marinade, in a food processor, combine all the sauce ingredients and pulse

until a purée forms. Reserve 1/4 cup marinade and place the remainder in a large resealable bag. Add duck breasts to the bag, turning to coat. Refrigerate for 20 minutes.

2. While duck marinates, preheat the grill to 425°F (218°C) using direct heat with a cast iron grate installed. Remove duck breasts from the marinade and place skin side down on the grate. Close the lid and grill until lightly brown, about 5 to 8 minutes. Flip breasts and grill until an instant-read thermometer inserted into the thickest part of a breast reads 165°F (74°C), about 10 to 12 minutes more.

3. Remove duck breasts from the grill, and serve immediately with the reserved 1/4 cup marinade and sliced scallions.

Honey And Spice Sautéed Pork Tacos

Servings:4
Cooking Time: 5 Minutes

Ingredients:
- 1 pound boneless pork chops, thinly-cut (1/2-inch thick), cut into strips
- 1 tablespoon honey
- 1 tablespoon olive oil
- 1 teaspoon lemon juice
- 1 teaspoon soy sauce
- ½ teaspoon ground chipotle pepper (smoked or plain paprika can be used as an alternative)
- 8 small corn tortillas, warmed
- 1 cup romaine lettuce, shredded
- 1 cup pico de gallo*
- Light sour cream to taste

Directions:
1. Preheat the grill to 400°F using direct heat with a cast iron grate installed.
2. In a medium sized bowl combine the honey, olive oil, lemon juice, soy sauce and ground chipotle pepper and whisk to combine. Add the sliced pork to the marinade and let it sit for 15 minutes.
3. Preheat the cast iron griddle on the cooking grid. Add the slices of pork to the skillet and cook for 1-2 minutes on each side, flipping with tongs in the middle of the cooking process. Once cooked, remove the pork to a plate and reserve.
4. Arrange 8 corn tortillas on a platter. Sprinkle each with equal amounts of shredded lettuce and pico de gallo. Arrange a few pieces of pork on top of each taco, and top with sour cream if desired.
5. You can find fresh pico de gallo, typically a combination of onions, chiles, tomatoes, lime juice and cilantro, in the refrigerated section of the produce department in most major supermarkets.

Turkey Bacon Dogs

Servings:8
Cooking Time: 20 Minutes

Ingredients:
- 8 Nature's Own 100% Whole Wheat Hot Dog Rolls
- 1 package (16 ounces) Butterball Bun Size Premium Turkey Franks
- 8 slices Butterball Turkey Bacon
- 1/2 to 3/4 cup shredded Cheddar or Monterey Jack cheese
- Salsa (medium or hot)
- Pickled jalapeño pepper slices (optional)

- Sour cream (optional)

Directions:

1. Preheat the grill to 500°F using direct heat with a cast iron grate installed.
2. Spray cold grate of grill with cooking spray. Wrap each turkey frank with 1 slice turkey bacon. Grill franks, turning frequently, until bacon is crisp.
3. Place franks in hot dog rolls. Immediately sprinkle with cheese. Serve with salsa and if desired, jalapeno pepper slices and sour cream.

Ham Muffinini

Servings:4
Cooking Time: 7 Minutes

Ingredients:

- 4 Nature's Own 100% Whole Wheat English Muffins, split
- 8 very thin asparagus spears
- 8 slices Swiss or Gruyere cheese
- ¼ pound sliced smoked ham
- Olive oil
- Salt
- Pepper
- Dijon mustard

Directions:

1. Preheat the grill to 400°F using direct heat with a cast iron grate installed.
2. Brush asparagus spears lightly with oil; season with salt and pepper. Place on the griddle; cook 3 minutes or until lightly charred. Cool slightly; cut each spear crosswise in half.
3. Meanwhile spread mustard over muffin halves. Layer each of 4 muffin halves with 1 slice cheese. Top evenly with ham, asparagus, remaining cheese and muffin

halves; press sandwiches together slightly. Brush outside of sandwiches lightly with oil.
4. Cook sandwiches on the griddle 3 to 4 minutes or until browned and cheese melts.

Pork Rib Roast Roulade

Servings:4
Cooking Time: 45 Minutes

Ingredients:

- 1 pork rib roast
- 1 tbsp Pine Street Market Summer Spice or your favorite pork seasoning
- 2 tsp kosher salt
- 1 bunch of parsley, chopped
- 1 orange, segmented
- 2 tsp capers
- 2 cloves garlic, minced
- 2 tbsp pickled mustard seeds (optional)

Directions:

1. Preheat the grill to 350°F using direct heat with a cast iron grate installed.
2. Cut the loin to unroll the meat. Season with half of the spice or pork seasoning and half of the salt. Add half of the parsley and orange segments; add the capers and garlic. Roll the loin back up and truss it with butcher twine using a surgeon's knot in-between each of the ribs. Season the outside of the pork with the remaining salt and seasoning.
3. Put the roast fat side up on the cooking grid and roast for 45 minutes to an hour or until the internal temperature reaches 145ºF. Remove from the kamado grill and let rest for 10 minutes. Remove the string and slice between the bones. Garnish with parsley, orange segments and pickled mustard seed. Enjoy!

BEEF

Brisket Poutine

Servings: 6
Cooking Time: 10 Minutes

Ingredients:

- One 10 to 12 lb (4.5 to 5.5 kg) whole packer brisket (Choice or higher)
- 1 cup (240 ml) coarsely ground pepper
- 1 cup (240 ml) non-iodized salt
- ¼ cup (60 ml) granulated garlic
- ¼ cup (60 ml) onion powder
- ¼ cup (60 ml) paprika
- French fries
- Cheese curds
- 6 Tbsp. unsalted butter
- ¼ cup unbleached all-purpose flour
- 20 oz. beef broth
- 10 oz. chicken broth
- Pepper, to taste

Directions:

1. Mix the rub ingredients in a large bowl. This mix will make more than you need for one brisket; store the remainder in an airtight container.

2. Trim the excess fat and silver skin from the brisket. Also, remove any "hard" pieces of fat as they will not render off during the cooking process. Trim the fat off the bottom of the brisket leaving only ¼ in (6 mm) fat. Apply rub to all sides of the meat liberally. Cover the brisket and place in the refrigerator to marinate overnight.

3. Preheat the grill to 250°F using direct heat with a cast iron grate installed.

4. Place the brisket on the grid, fat-side down – this is my preference, but highly debated in the barbecue world. Fat-side up is fine if that is your preference, but fat down is what many competitors do as it gives you a much better presentation. When the meat reaches an internal temperature of 160°F, double wrap the brisket in non-waxed butcher paper or aluminum foil – this is what we call the Texas crutch. The bark will have formed nicely by this point.

5. Continue to smoke the brisket until the meat is "probe tender," which means when you probe it there is no resistance. Each piece of meat is different but this will likely be at an internal temperature of between 200-202°F. Remove the brisket from the grill, wrap in a towel and place in a cooler for at least one hour. This will allow the juices to re-distribute in the meat. Unwrap the brisket and slice against the grain.

6. Prepare the gravy: In a small bowl, dissolve the cornstarch in the water and set aside. In a large saucepan, melt the butter. Add the flour to create the roux and cook, stirring regularly, for about 5 minutes, until the mixture turns golden brown. Add the beef and chicken broth and bring to a boil, stirring with a whisk. Stir in the cornstarch and simmer for 3 to 5 minutes or until the sauce thickens. Season to taste with salt and pepper. Prepare French fries, chop brisket. Top French fries with brisket, French fries, cheese curds, and gravy.

Beer Can Bbq Burgers

Servings: 4
Cooking Time: 30 Minutes

Ingredients:

- ½ medium white onion
- 2lb (1kg) ground chuck
- ¼ cup cooked wild rice
- 3 tbsp sweet paprika
- 2 tbsp Dijon mustard
- 2 tbsp minced garlic
- 2 tbsp kosher salt, plus more as needed
- 2 tbsp ground black pepper, plus more as needed
- 9 tbsp smoky BBQ sauce, divided
- 4 tbsp sweet pepper relish
- 4 tbsp prepared horseradish
- 4 hamburger buns
- to serve
- lettuce leaves
- tomato slices
- onion slices

Directions:

1. Preheat the grill to 400 °F (163°C) using indirect heat with a cast iron grate installed. Place onion on the grate, close the lid, and grill until beginning to soften and char, about 7 to 10 minutes. Remove onion from the grill and dice. Set aside.
2. In a large bowl, use your hands to combine beef, cooked rice, paprika, mustard, garlic, salt, pepper, and 1 tbsp BBQ sauce. Form the mixture into 4 patties, and press a can of beer or soda into the middle of each patty to create an indentation. Season the patties with salt and pepper, and fill the indentations with the grilled onion and relish, evenly dividing the filling ingredients among the 4 patties. Top each burger with 1 tbsp BBQ sauce.
3. Place the patties on the grate, close the lid, and grill until the internal temperature reaches 155°F (68°C), about 8 to 12 minutes. Don't move or flip the burgers.
4. In a small bowl, combine horseradish and remaining 4 tbsp BBQ sauce. Remove the burgers from the grill and let rest for a few minutes. While the burgers rest, place the bun halves cut side down on the grate and toast for 3 to 5 minutes.
5. Spread the bottom buns with the BBQ horseradish mixture. Place a patty on each bottom bun, top with lettuce, tomato, and onion, and place the top buns. Serve immediately.

Smoked Brisket

Servings:16
Cooking Time: 640 Minutes

Ingredients:

- 1 6-9 lbs. brisket (best available preferably Wagyu)
- 1 cup salt
- 1 cup ground black pepper
- ¼ cup garlic powder
- ¼ cup Paprika
- ¼ cup ground white pepper
- ¼ cup white sugar
- ¼ cup ground mustard

Directions:

1. Preheat the grill to 275°F using direct heat with a cast iron grate installed.

2. Trim excess fat off brisket to make smooth-even surface. Mix all the dry ingredients together and rub the brisket well with the seasoning mix (reserve any remaining for future brisket).

3. Cook the brisket until the internal temperature reaches 203°F. This usually takes 8-12 hours. Your brisket will hit a "stall" somewhere during the cook; you will notice the internal temperature increasing quickly and then plateauing when moisture starts to form on the outside of the brisket. Be patient – it can take a few hours to get past this stage. To speed up the cooking and reduce the darkness of the outer bark you can wrap the brisket in butcher paper and put back on the grill.

4. When the brisket hits 203°F drop it from 3 above a cutting board. The brisket should not bounce, rather it could settle on the board with a "jiggle". This is the best way to test that all of the connective tissue has been fully cooked down and that the brisket will be tender.

Surf And Turf Rolls

Servings:8
Cooking Time: 60 Minutes

Ingredients:
- 1 lb (450 g) beef tenderloin
- 8 shrimp or prawns (size 8/12 count)
- 1 clove of garlic, peeled and finely chopped
- Olive oil
- 2 1/2 cups (40 g) rocket (arugula)
- 3 oz (85 g) dried tomatoes
- 7 oz (200 g) pig caul, thoroughly washed*
- Lime juice

- 4 Cobs in Husks
- Butter
- Finely shredded zest of 1/2 lemon
- 2 egg yolks
- 2 tbsp (30 ml) wholegrain mustard
- 1 dash white balsamic vinegar
- 3.5 oz (100 ml) vegetable oil
- 1.75 oz (50 ml) olive oil
- 1 passion fruit
- 1 tablespoon sour cream
- Juice of 1/2 lemon

Directions:
1. Preheat the grill to 210°F using direct heat with a cast iron grate installed.

2. Cut the beef tenderloin into four equal portions. Wrap each piece of meat in plastic wrap and flatten with the underside of a frying pan.

3. Peel the prawns, remove the intestine and rinse with water. In a bowl, coat the prawns with some olive oil, plus the garlic and salt and pepper to taste. Wash the rocket and slice the tomatoes.

4. Remove the meat from the wrap and distribute the rocket and tomato slices over the meat. Place 2 prawns in the center of each piece of meat, roll up tightly and wrap in a piece of pork caul or secure with toothpicks. Put the rolls on the cooking grid, close the lid and cook for 20 minutes.

5. Remove the rolls from the grid and cover with foil. Using a Pit Mitt or barbecue mitt, carefully add the platesetter and replace the Cast Iron Grid; heat the kamado grill to 350°F.

6. Take the cobs and the rolls off the grill. Remove the husk and silk and spread the cobs immediately with butter.

7. Cut the rolls into slices and drizzle with lime juice. Divide across the plates and serve with the mayonnaise and a delicious rocket salad.

8. Keeping the husks intact, snip the silks from the top of the corn and moisten the cobs in water. Place the cobs on the grid and grill for about 35 minutes, turning regularly until the husk has blackened evenly. For the final 5 minutes of the preparation time add the rolls and cook until nice and brown.

9. Prepare the mayonnaise by blending together the egg yolks, mustard, lemon zest and balsamic vinegar. Stirring all the time, pour in the vegetable oil and olive oil, one drop at a time and then in a small trickle, to create a creamy mayonnaise. Cut the passion fruit in half, scoop out the flesh and mix with the sour cream. Add to the mayonnaise along with the lemon juice and salt and pepper to taste.

Beef Short Ribs

Servings:4
Cooking Time: 300 Minutes

Ingredients:
- 3-4 lbs. beef short ribs
- Ancho Chili & Coffee Seasoning
- 4 tbsp Habanero Hot Sauce

Directions:
1. Preheat the grill to 250°F using direct heat with a cast iron grate installed.

2. Coat the short ribs with the Habanero hot sauce; the sauce will act as a binder to allow the seasoning to adhere better to the ribs. Apply a liberal amount of Ancho Chile & Coffee Seasoning to the ribs. Allow the ribs to sit at room temperature for 15 minutes; this will allow the rub to penetrate the ribs and adding the amazing flavors.

3. Smoke the ribs for 5 hours. After 5 hours begin to check the internal temperature; once the internal temperature of the ribs reaches 198°F remove the ribs from the kamado grill and wrap them in butcher paper or foil for at least an hour to allow the moisture to redistribute.

4. Enjoy those ribs; you've worked hard for them!

Holiday Sirloin Roast

Servings: 6
Cooking Time:180 Minutes

Ingredients:
- 1 (5-8 lb) sirloin roast
- 1/4 cup Dijon mustard
- 2 Tablespoons fresh rosemary, chopped
- 1/2 tsp salt
- 1/4 tsp pepper
- 3 cloves garlic, minced

Directions:
1. Bring the roast to room temperature for 30 minutes before cooking.
2. Sprinkle the roast with salt and pepper.
3. Spread liberally with Dijon and press rosemary and garlic into the mustard.
4. Grilling:

5. Preheat the grill to 325°F using direct heat with a cast iron grate installed.

6. Place the roast directly on the grid and close the dome for 2 1/2 to 3 hours or until the internal temperature reaches 130°F.

7. Remove from the grill onto a board and allow it to rest for 20 minutes before carving.

Reverse-sear Ribeye

Servings: 4
Cooking Time: 80 Minutes

Ingredients:
- 2lb (1kg) ribeye steak
- 1 tbsp vegetable oil
- kosher salt and freshly ground black pepper
- for the sauce
- 3 red bell peppers, left whole
- 1/2 bunch of scallions, trimmed
- 1/3 cup whole almonds
- 3 large garlic cloves
- 1/2 tsp crushed red pepper flakes
- 2 tbsp lemon juice
- 1/2 tsp kosher salt
- 1/4 cup extra virgin olive oil
- to smoke
- pecan or bourbon barrel wood chunks

Directions:
1. Preheat the grill to 225°F (107°C). Once hot, add the wood chunks and install the heat deflector and a standard grate with a cast iron skillet on the grate.

2. In the hot skillet, place almonds and toast until golden brown, about 10 to 15 minutes, stirring occasionally. Remove the skillet from the grill and set aside.

3. Rub steak with oil, season with salt and pepper to taste, and place on the grate. Smoke until the internal temperature reaches 115°F (46°C), about 30 minutes per pound (approximately 1 hour per kilogram). Transfer to a platter and set aside.

4. Remove the heat deflector, replace the standard grate with a cast iron grate, and open the top and bottom vents to raise the grill temperature to 500°F (260°C) using direct heat. Place peppers and scallions on the grate, and grill until beginning to soften and char, about 3 minutes per side, turning once. Remove from the grill, seed and roughly chop the peppers, and roughly chop the scallions.

5. To make the sauce, in a food processor, combine almonds, garlic, and red pepper flakes, and pulse until finely ground. Add peppers, scallions, lemon juice, and salt, and purée, adding oil in a slow stream. Season with black pepper to taste.

6. Place steak on the grate and sear until steak reaches your desired level of doneness, about 2 to 3 minutes per side for medium rare. Transfer to a cutting board and thinly slice. Top with the romesco sauce, and serve immediately.

Ray's Herb Butter Prime Rib

Servings:6
Cooking Time: 120 Minutes

Ingredients:
- 5 pound boneless ribeye roast
- Kosher salt
- Black pepper, coarse ground
- 2 sticks of butter, at room temperature

- 4 cloves garlic, crushed
- ¼ cup chopped fresh thyme leaves
- ¼ cup chopped fresh tarragon leaves
- ¼ cup chopped fresh parsley
- Au Jus and Horseradish Sauce for serving

Directions:

1. Preheat the grill to 325°F using direct heat with a cast iron grate installed. Season the roast liberally with the salt and pepper. In a medium bowl, mix together the butter, garlic, and herbs. Spread the herb butter evenly all over the roast. Place roast on the cooking grid. Cook it until it reaches an internal temperature of 125°F in the center for medium rare. This will take about 1½ to 2 hours. Remove to a platter and tent loosely with foil. Let rest for 15 minutes. Slice thick for prime rib type slabs or thin for a roast beef presentation.

Smoked Goat Bolognese

Servings: 8
Cooking Time: 150 Minutes

Ingredients:

- 1½lb (680g) boneless goat leg
- kosher salt and freshly ground black pepper
- 1–2 tsp sweet smoked paprika
- 1 medium yellow onion, chopped
- 4 garlic cloves, chopped
- 3 celery stalks, diced
- 2 carrots, diced
- 1½ cups beer
- 1½ cups cola
- 1lb (450g) dried rigatoni
- olive oil
- for the sauce

- 1 tbsp olive oil
- 1 white onion, diced
- 4 garlic cloves, minced
- 15oz (425g) can crushed tomatoes
- 1 cup red wine
- 1 tsp fresh oregano, minced
- ½ cup heavy cream
- to smoke
- cherry or wine barrel wood chunks

Directions:

1. About 2 to 3 hours before cooking, coat goat leg liberally with salt, pepper, and a light (but thorough) dusting of paprika. Cover with plastic wrap and allow to come to room temperature.
2. Preheat the grill to 250°F (121°C). Once hot, add the wood chunks, then install the heat deflector and a standard grate with a dutch oven on the grate. Add onion, garlic, celery, and carrots to the dutch oven. Close the grill lid and sweat the vegetables for 5 minutes. Stir in beer and cola, and add goat leg.
3. Loosely cover the dutch oven with aluminum foil, close the grill lid, and smoke until the internal temperature reaches 190°F (88°C), about 1 to 2 hours, checking the temperature every hour. Transfer goat leg to a large serving platter and let rest for 30 to 45 minutes, then shred the meat. Season with salt and pepper to taste. Set aside.
4. Cook the rigatoni on the stovetop according to package directions. Drain and rinse with cold water, and toss with a little olive oil to prevent sticking. Set aside.

5. To make the sauce, on the stovetop in a large skillet over medium heat, heat oil until shimmering. Add onions and garlic, and sauté until fragrant and beginning to brown, about 2 to 3 minutes. Add tomatoes, wine, and oregano. Cook until reduced by one-fourth, about 10 to 15 minutes.

6. Add shredded meat, cream, and cooked rigatoni to the skillet. Stir gently and cook until thick, about 5 to 7 minutes. Season with salt and pepper to taste, and serve warm.

Smoked Beef Tenderloin

Servings: 8
Cooking Time: 120 Minutes

Ingredients:

- 1 whole beef tenderloin, about 5lb (2.3kg) in total, trimmed
- 1⁄4 cup extra virgin olive oil
- kosher salt and freshly ground black pepper
- 4 garlic cloves, minced
- 1⁄4 cup chopped fresh basil
- 1⁄4 cup chopped fresh rosemary
- 1⁄4 cup chopped fresh oregano
- 1⁄4 cup chopped fresh marjoram
- 1⁄4 cup chopped fresh flat-leaf parsley
- 8 hoagie rolls, to serve
- for the sauce
- 2 tbsp mustard seeds
- 1⁄4 cup Dijon mustard
- 1⁄4 cup whole grain mustard
- 5 tbsp mayonnaise
- 5 tbsp sour cream
- 21⁄4 tsp Worcestershire sauce
- to smoke
- alder, hickory, or apricot wood chunks

Directions:

1. Rub beef with oil, salt, pepper, garlic, basil, rosemary, oregano, marjoram, and parsley. Wrap tightly with plastic wrap and refrigerate for 4 to 24 hours.

2. To make the sauce, in a medium bowl, combine mustard seeds, Dijon mustard, whole grain mustard, mayonnaise, sour cream, and Worcestershire sauce. Cover the bowl and refrigerate for 1 hour or overnight to allow the flavors to meld.

3. Preheat the grill to 225°F (107°C). Once hot, add the wood chunks and install the heat deflector and a standard grate. Place tenderloin on the grate, close the lid, and smoke until the internal temperature reaches 125°F (52°C), about 1 to 2 hours.

4. Transfer beef to a cutting board and let rest for 15 minutes. While the meat rests, place rolls on the grate cut side down and lightly toast, about 2 to 3 minutes. Thinly slice the meat. To serve, spread the mustard cream sauce on the rolls and pile on the beef.

Reverse Seared Ribeyes

Servings:4
Cooking Time: 5 Minutes

Ingredients:

- 2 ribeye steaks, at least 2 inches thick
- Classic Steakhouse Seasoning
- Roasted Garlic, Basil & Parsley Banner Butter

Directions:

1. Preheat the grill to 250°F using direct heat with a cast iron grate installed.

2. Bring the ribeyes to room temperature and season all sides liberally with Classic Steakhouse Seasoning. Connect the kamado grill Genius for 250°F kamado grill temperature and 125°F meat temperature. Remove the steak when the internal temperature reaches 125°F. Disconnect the kamado grill Genius.
3. Set the kamado grill for direct cooking without a platesetter at 550°F.
4. Sear each side of the steak for 1 minute. Remove the steak from the kamado grill when the internal temperature reaches 135°F. Smear the steak with herb butter (we used Roasted Garlic, Basil & Parsley Banner Butter) and let rest for 10 minutes. Slice and enjoy!

Pimento Cheese Burger With Bacon Jam

Servings:4
Cooking Time: 12 Minutes

Ingredients:

- 4 Nature's Own 100% Whole Wheat Buns
- 4 seasoned burger patties
- 1 cup prepared pimento cheese spread
- 1-2 sliced plum tomatoes
- 2 cups romaine lettuce
- 1/2 cup sweet onion slices
- 1 cup crumbled bacon pieces
- 3 tablespoons maple syrup
- 1 tablespoon balsamic vinegar glaze

Directions:

1. In a food processor, mix the bacon, maple syrup and balsamic glaze until it is fully incorporated to make the bacon jam. It will look like a textured spread, then set aside.
2. Preheat the grill to 400°F using direct heat with a cast iron grate installed.
3. Cook burgers 5-6 minutes per side to desired temperature.
4. Layer bun with burger, pimento cheese, lettuce, onion, tomato and bacon jam. Top burger with bun top and serve.

Sloppy Joes

Servings: 4
Cooking Time: 40 Minutes

Ingredients:

- 1 lb ground beef
- 1/4 cup onion, finely chopped
- 1/4 cup bell pepper, finely chopped
- 1 clove garlic, finely chopped
- 1/2 cup tomato sauce
- 1/4 cup ketchup
- 2 Tablespoons brown sugar
- 1 Tablespoon brown mustard
- Salt & Pepper

Directions:

1. Preheat the grill to 400°F using direct heat with a cast iron grate installed with the dutch oven on the grid.
2. Place all ingredients in the dutch oven and stir.
3. Cover the dutch oven and lower the dome for 30-40 minutes or until the beef is cooked through.
4. Serve on hamburger buns.

Seared Bison Filet

Servings:6
Cooking Time: 10 Minutes

Ingredients:

- 8 oz bison filet
- 1 tsp salt
- 1 tsp pepper

Directions:

1. Preheat the grill to 500°F using direct heat with a cast iron grate installed with grillspander platesetter Basket in place for raised direct cooking.
2. Bring the bison to room temperature and season with salt and pepper. Place the filet on the cooking grid and grill for 5 minutes per side. Remove from the kamado grill when the internal temperature reaches 125°F.
3. Let rest 5 minutes before slicing and serving.

Big Beef Ribs With Beer

Servings:4
Cooking Time: 240 Minutes

Ingredients:

- 1 Rack Beef Plate Short Ribs, 3-4 bones and 5-6 pounds
- Olive oil
- Kosher salt
- Black pepper, coarsely ground
- Granulated garlic
- 1 bottle dark beer

Directions:

1. Preheat the grill to 265°F using direct heat with a cast iron grate installed. Peel the membrane from the bone side of the ribs.

Brush the ribs all over with a light coating of olive oil. Season liberally with salt and pepper and lightly with the granulated garlic.
2. Place the ribs directly on the cooking grate bone side down and cook for 2 hours. Flip the ribs and cook for another hour or until the ribs are deep golden brown.
3. Place the ribs in a foil pan and pour the beer over them. Cover tightly with foil and return to the grill. Continue cooking until the ribs are very tender to the touch and have reached an internal temp of at least 200°. The ribs will shrink quite a bit. This should take another 2-3 hours but they're not done until they are very tender.
4. Remove the ribs from the pan and cut into individual bones. Serve whole or cut into serving sized pieces. Serve with white bread, pickles, raw onion slices and barbecue sauce on the side.

Venison Casserole

Servings:12
Cooking Time: 60 Minutes

Ingredients:

- 1 pound bulk venison sausage
- 6 English muffins cut into 1 inch cubes
- ¼ cup butter, melted
- 1 cup shredded cheddar cheese
- 1 cup shredded mozzarella cheese
- ½ red onion, finely chopped
- 1 small green pepper, finely chopped
- 12 eggs
- 2 cups milk
- 1/2 tsp salt
- 1/2 tsp pepper

- 1 teaspoon paprika

Directions:

1. Cook the sausage over medium heat in a skillet thoroughly breaking it up as you cook. Set aside to cool.
2. Preheat the grill to 350°F using direct heat with a cast iron grate installed. In a greased Deep Dish Pizza/Baking Stone or a 13 x 9 grill-friendly baking dish, laycr half the muffin cubes and half the cooked sausage. Repeat layers. Top with onions and red pepper. Drizzle with butter and top with the cheese.
3. In a large bowl, combine the eggs, milk, salt and pepper. Pour over casserole. Sprinkle with paprika. Let rest for at least 30 minutes for everything to soak in, or do this the night before and refrigerate for up to 12 hours. (If you do refrigerate the casserole remove it at least 30 minutes before cooking to warm up)
4. Bake uncovered for about an hour, or until a knife inserted into the center comes out clean. Let stand 5 minutes.

Short Ribs & Polenta

Servings: 4
Cooking Time: 200 Minutes

Ingredients:
- 8 beef short ribs
- 6 slices bacon, diced
- 3 carrots, diced
- 2 cloves garlic, minced
- 1 onion, diced
- 4 cups beef broth
- 1/2 cup red wine
- 1/4 cup flour
- 1 Tablespoon tomato paste
- 1/2 tsp ground fennel
- 2 sprigs fresh thyme
- 2 sprigs fresh rosemary
- Salt and Pepper
- 4 cups water
- 4 cups milk
- 2 cups polenta
- 1/2 cup sour cream
- 1/2 cup parmesan cheese, grated
- 3 Tablespoons butter
- 2 tsp salt

Directions:

1. Season the short ribs with salt and pepper and lightly dredge in the flour.
2. Place the bacon in a cold dutch oven over medium heat on the stove top.
3. Remove the bacon when it becomes crispy and set aside.
4. Working in batches, brown the short ribs on all sides. Set aside.
5. Remove all but 2 Tablespoon of the fat.
6. Add carrots, onion, and garlic and cook until soft.
7. Add tomato paste and cook for 2 minutes.
8. Add red wine and scrape the bottom of the dutch oven for 1 minute.
9. Add back bacon and beef, stir in fennel, thyme, and rosemary.
10. When there is 40 minutes left, bring the water, butter, and milk for the polenta to a simmer in a large sauce pan.
11. Add the salt and polenta to the water mixture and whisk constantly for 3-4 minutes.

12. Simmer partially covered for 45 minutes, stirring every 10 minutes.
13. Add sour cream and parmesan to the polenta and stir. Keep the polenta covered until you are ready to serve.
14. Grilling:
15. Preheat the grill to 325°F using direct heat with a cast iron grate installed.
16. Cover the dutch oven and transfer to the grill.
17. Close the dome for 2 1/2 hours.
18. When the ribs have been in the grill for 2 1/2 hours, close all the vents and allow the dutch oven to sit inside the grill for another 20 minutes.
19. Remove the dutch oven from the grill, remove stems from the herbs, and skim any fat that has come to the surface.
20. Serve two short ribs on a bed of creamy polenta.

Dr. Bbq's Smoked Flat-cut Brisket With Coffee

Servings:2
Cooking Time: 60 Minutes

Ingredients:
- 1 USDA Choice flat-cut brisket (5 to 6 pounds), fat left on
- Barbecue Rub #67
- ½ cup strong brewed coffee
- ½ cup Sugar in the Raw
- ½ cup kosher salt
- 3 tablespoons chili powder
- 3 tablespoons paprika
- 1 teaspoon garlic powder
- 1 teaspoon onion powder
- ½ teaspoon black pepper
- ½ teaspoon lemon pepper
- ½ teaspoon ground coffee
- ¼ teaspoon cayenne pepper

Directions:
1. Preheat the grill to 235°F using direct heat with a cast iron grate installed.
2. Season the brisket liberally with the rub. Cook the brisket fat-side down for 1 hour and then flip it to fat-side up. Cook to an internal temperature of 160°F.
3. Lay out a big double-thick layer of heavy-duty aluminum foil and lay the brisket on it fat-side up. Pull up the sides of the foil and pour on the coffee as you close up the package. Be careful not to puncture it or you'll have to start over. Return the brisket to the cooker. After another hour, begin checking the internal temperature. When it reaches 200°F, remove the brisket and let it rest for 30 minutes, wrapped. Remove the brisket from the foil. It desired, skim the fat from the liquid and serve the remaining juices as a sauce. Slice the brisket about ¼ inch thick to serve.
4. Combine all the ingredients in a medium bowl and mix well. The rub may be stored in an airtight container in a cool place for up to 6 months.

Beef & Lamb Sliders

Servings: 12
Cooking Time: 15 Minutes

Ingredients:
- 1½lb (450g) 80% lean ground beef
- 1lb (680g) ground lamb

- kosher salt and freshly ground black pepper
- 1 tbsp dried marjoram
- for the sauce
- 6 cornichon pickles, coarsely chopped
- 4 tbsp coarsely chopped fresh flat-leaf parsley
- 1 tbsp drained capers
- 4 garlic cloves, peeled
- 1 tsp ground cayenne pepper
- 1/2 cup mayonnaise
- 2 tbsp whole grain mustard
- to serve
- 12 slider buns
- 4oz (110g) paneer cheese, cut into 12 thick slices
- 2 large Roma tomatoes, thickly sliced

Directions:

1. To make the sauce, in a food processor, place cornichons, parsley, capers, and garlic, and pulse until finely chopped. Add cayenne, mayonnaise, and mustard, and pulse until blended.
2. In a large bowl, gently combine beef and lamb, and season well with salt and pepper. Add 2 tbsp of the cornichon and caper sauce to the meat, and gently mix. Form the mixture into 12 equally sized patties and make a slight indentation in the center of each with your thumb.
3. Preheat the grill to 400°F (204°C) using direct heat with a cast iron grate installed. Place the bun halves on the grate cut side down and grill for 1 minute. Transfer buns, cut side up, to a work surface, and spread the bottom half of each bun with a spoonful of the remaining cornichon and caper sauce.

4. Place the patties on the grate, close the lid, and grill until charred on the bottom, about 4 minutes. Flip the sliders and grill until the internal temperature reaches 155°F (68°C), about 4 minutes more. Transfer the burgers to the toasted buns and let rest for 5 minutes.
5. Place the paneer slices on the grate and grill until soft, about 2 minutes per side. Top the sliders with grilled paneer and sliced tomatoes. Serve immediately.

Smash Cheese Burgers

Servings:4
Cooking Time: 5 Minutes

Ingredients:

- 1 lb ground beef
- 1 tbsp garlic powder
- Salt and pepper to taste
- 8 slices of cheddar cheese, optional

Directions:

1. Preheat the grill to 500°F using direct heat with a cast iron grate installed.
2. Season the beef with garlic powder, salt and pepper. Roll beef into 8 – 2 oz. balls.
3. Place 4 balls on the plancha, close the lid and wait 1-2 minutes. Open the lid and smash the balls with a spatula until they are about an inch thick. Cook 2 minutes. Flip the burgers and cook another 2 minutes. Put cheese on the burger and wait another minute, until the cheese is melted. Repeat with the remaining balls.
4. Top with your favorite toppings.

Tyler Farr's Venison Cube Steak

Servings:4
Cooking Time: 5 Minutes

Ingredients:

- 2 pounds venison cube steak
- 2 cans Diet Coke
- ½ teaspoon garlic powder
- ½ teaspoon black pepper
- 1 teaspoon salt
- ¼ cup prepared mustard
- 1 cup flour
- 2 cups vegetable oil

Directions:

1. Place the cube venison into a large bowl; cover with Diet Coke. You can add multiple steaks at the same time, but be sure to cover the meat completely with the liquid before adding more venison to the bowl. Let sit for at least one hour and then turn the venison inside the bowl. Flip the venison steaks inside the bowl and allow them to sit for another hour, or even overnight.
2. Remove the cube venison from the Diet Coke and pat dry with a paper towel. Season on both sides with salt, pepper and garlic pepper. Coat each venison steak with a light covering of prepared mustard, then dredge in flour and let rest about ten minutes.
3. Preheat the grill to 350°F using direct heat with a cast iron grate installed.
4. Heat a dutch oven or a cast iron skillet for approximately 5 minutes, add the vegetable oil and allow it to heat. Add the venison in a single layer; flip when the batter turns brown around the edges. The venison cube steaks should cook for about three minutes on both sides.

Wild Mushroom And Blue Cheese Stuffed Burger

Servings:4
Cooking Time: 10 Minutes

Ingredients:

- 2 lbs (900 g) ground venison or sirloin
- Salt and pepper, for seasoning
- 2 1⁄2 tbsp (37 ml) hot sauce
- 10 oz (285 g) mixed wild mushrooms, sautéed and drained
- 8 oz (115 g) blue cheese, crumbled
- Arugula for garnish

Directions:

1. Mix the hot sauce into the ground meat, then divide the meat into eight equal portions, 1⁄4 pound (113 g) each. Take one of the divided ground meat and form it in a small cup.
2. Fill center with the mushrooms and 6 oz (90 g) blue cheese. Place remaining ground meat on top and seal.
3. Preheat the grill to 400°F using direct heat with a cast iron grate installed. Cook burgers for 3 to 5 minutes per side depending on desired doneness. Top with remaining blue cheese and arugula.

Italian Sausage Sliders

Servings:16
Cooking Time: 6 Minutes

Ingredients:

- 2 pounds Johnsonville All Natural Ground Italian Sausage or Links (remove from casing)
- 1 pound ground beef
- 16 small slider buns or mini sandwich rolls
- Condiments
- Provolone cheese and Marinara sauce
- Fresh mozzarella, fresh basil, and sliced tomatoes
- Giardiniera – marinated chopped vegetables and olives
- Sauteed onions and roasted red peppers
- Sauteed mushrooms and Cheddar cheese

Directions:

1. Preheat the grill to 400°F using direct heat with a cast iron grate installed.
2. In a large bowl, combine sausage and beef. Using your hands, blend the two meats together and form into one large ball. Use a spoon or a small measuring cup to gather up about a 3 ounce ball and press into patties … with the Mini Burger Basket you can form and cook 12 Mini Burgers at once!
3. Place the Mini Burger Basket or individual sliders directly on the cooking grid. Cook for about 3 minutes then flip and continue cooking for another 3 minutes. The internal temperature should be 160°F.
4. Slice the buns and top the sliders with your favorite condiments.

Asian Flank Steak

Servings: 4
Cooking Time: 14 Minutes

Ingredients:

- 1 (1 1/2 –pound) flank steak
- 1 recipe Spicy Thai Marinade

Directions:

1. Pour marinade into a large zip top bag and place steak inside. Refrigerate at least 30 minutes or up to overnight.
2. Remove the meat from the fridge while you preheat the grill to 500°F using direct heat with a cast iron grate installed.
3. Grilling:
4. Place flank steak on the grid and close the dome for 3 minutes.
5. Flip the steak over and cook an additional 2 minutes.
6. Close all of the vents and let the steak sit for 5 minutes or until the internal temperature reaches 130°F.
7. Remove the steak and allow it to rest for 10 minutes before slicing thinly on the bias.

Brisket Burnt Ends

Servings:8
Cooking Time: 120 Minutes

Ingredients:

- Full packer brisket
- Meat Church Holy Cow
- Kansas City Style Sweet & Smoky BBQ Sauce
- Your favorite clover honey

Directions:

1. Preheat the grill to 275°F using direct heat with a cast iron grate installed. I recommend a heavier smoking wood chunks for this cook such as oak, hickory, mesquite, or pecan.

2. Trim the excess fat and silver skin from the brisket. Also, remove any "hard" pieces of fat as they will not render off during the cooking process. Trim the fat off the bottom of the brisket leaving only ¼ in (6 mm) fat.

3. A brisket is comprised of two muscles; the point (the fat end) and the flat (the lean end). In order to be able to cook brisket burnt ends you need to butcher the brisket a bit more than you would for a traditional packer. Therefore, after your traditional brisket butchering, you need to start to separate the flat form the point. Using a sharp boning knife expose the point meat so it can absorb smoke. You don't have to completely separate the muscles.

4. Place the brisket in the kamado grill fat-side down. When the meat reaches an internal temperature of 160°F, double wrap the brisket in non-waxed butcher paper or aluminum foil. The bark will have formed nicely by this point.

5. Continue to smoke the brisket until it reaches an internal temperature of 195°F. The brisket is not completely done at this point but we need to separate the point to make burnt ends. Unwrap the brisket and separate the point from the flat. Re-wrap the flat and return it to your grill. Continue to smoke it until the meat is "probe tender" which means when you probe it with an instant read thermometer there is no resistance. Think of a toothpick in a cake. Each piece of meat is different but this will likely be between an internal temperature around 203° F. Rest your brisket flat in a cooler for at least one hour.

6. Take the point and cut it into 1" cubes. Place the cubes in the aluminum pan. Season and toss the cubes with more Meat Church Holy Cow. Cover the cubes with Kansas City Style Sweet & Smoky BBQ sauce. Drizzle honey across the top. Finally, toss the cubes thoroughly to ensure they are completely covered. Return the pan to the grill and cook for another 1 – 2 hours or until all liquid has reduced and caramelized.

7. Allow to cool for a few minutes and enjoy immediately!

Smoked Beef Brisket

Servings: 38
Cooking Time: 900 Minutes

Ingredients:

- 1¼ cups sugar
- 2⁄3 cup ground black pepper
- 2⁄3 cup seasoned salt
- 2⁄3 cup kosher salt
- 2½ tbsp ground cayenne pepper
- 15lb (6.8kg) whole beef brisket, trimmed of fat
- pickle slices (optional), to serve
- BBQ sauce (optional), to serve
- to smoke
- post oak, hickory, or mesquite wood chunks

Directions:

1. In a medium bowl, combine sugar, pepper, seasoned salt, kosher salt, and cayenne. Rub brisket with the seasoning mixture. Wrap tightly with plastic wrap and refrigerate for 24 hours.
2. Preheat the grill to 225°F (107°C). Once hot, add the wood chunks, install the heat deflector, place a drip pan on top, and install a standard grate. Remove brisket from the fridge and allow to come to room temperature.
3. Place the brisket fat side up on the grate, close the lid, and smoke until the internal temperature reaches 160°F (71°C), about 5 to 7 hours. Remove brisket from the grill, wrap heavily in aluminum foil, and return to the grill to continue to cook until the internal temperature reaches 185°F (85°C), about 8 hours. (Check the texture of the meat for doneness throughout the cooking process). The total cook time is about 15 hours, or 1 hour per pound (approximately 2 hours per kilogram).
4. Transfer brisket to a serving platter and let rest for 20 minutes. Slice or shred the meat, and serve with pickle slices and BBQ sauce (if desired).

Grilled Cheesesteak Pizza

Servings:4
Cooking Time: 8 Minutes

Ingredients:

- 1 tablespoon extra-virgin olive oil
- 1 roasted red bell pepper, sliced
- 1/2 onion, sliced
- 1 (14.5 ounce) can Red Gold Diced Tomatoes, drained
- 1/2 tablespoon dried oregano
- 5 ounces Laura's Lean Beef Sirloin Steak, cooked and thinly sliced
- 1-10 to 11 ounce container pizza dough, your favorite recipe or store bought
- 2 tablespoons Red Gold Tomato Paste
- 2 ounces shredded provolone cheese
- 2 ounces shredded low-fat cheddar cheese
- 1 tablespoon chopped fresh parsley

Directions:

1. Preheat the grill to 600°F using direct heat with a cast iron grate installed.
2. Heat olive oil in a Cast Iron Skillet. Add the red bell pepper, onions and tomatoes (reserve ¼ cup of the tomatoes) and cook together until onions are soft. Remove from the skillet, sprinkle with oregano and set aside.
3. In the skillet, grill steaks to desired temperature. Remove the skillet from the grill, slice the steak into thin pieces.
4. Add the platesetter for indirect cooking and reduce the heat to 450°F. Preheat a Pizza & Baking Stone.
5. Divide pizza dough in half and roll each half out into a circle on a Dough Rolling Mat, getting it as thin as possible.
6. Gently lay one of the crusts onto the Stone. Cook about 1 to 2 minutes per side, depending on temperature of grill. Use tongs to flip and cook each side of the crust. If bubbles appear, just prick the dough bubble and keep cooking. Repeat for the second crust.
7. Spread 1 tablespoon of tomato paste on each crust. Divide and top each pizza with the tomato mixture, beef and cheese. Carefully

return one pizza to the Stone. Cook an additional 3 to 4 minutes until cheese is melted. Repeat for the second pizza (keep a close watch on pizzas, removing if the crust is getting toasty).

8. Sprinkle with the 1/4 cup tomatoes that were set aside along with the fresh parsley. Serve immediately.

Justin Moore Rib-eye

Servings:4
Cooking Time: 38 Minutes

Ingredients:

- 4 (1-inch-thick) rib-eye steaks (also see how to pick the perfect steaks click here)
- 1/4 cup olive oil
- Kosher salt and freshly ground black pepper
- Sweet Onion & Garlic Butter
- 8 tablespoons unsalted butter
- 1 tablespoon finely minced garlic
- 1/4 cup minced sweet onions
- 1 tablespoon minced fresh parsley
- Kosher salt and freshly ground black pepper

Directions:

1. Set the kamado grill for direct cooking with the Cast Iron Grid.
2. Preheat the grill to 550°F using direct heat with a cast iron grate installed.
3. Using a basting brush, lightly coat each of the rib-eye steaks with the olive oil, season with salt and pepper, and set aside.
4. To make the garlic butter, melt the butter in a small saucepan on the stovetop. When the butter begins to foam, add the garlic and cook for 2 minutes, being careful not to let the garlic brown. Remove the pan from

the heat, add the onions, and stir. Let the butter cool for 30 minutes. Add the parsley, season with salt and pepper, and mix well.

5. Pour equal amounts of the mixture into 2 small bowls, reserving one for basting and one for serving.
6. Place the steaks on the Grid, baste with some of the garlic butter, and close the lid of the grill. Cook for 3 minutes. Turn the steaks over and baste with more garlic butter.
7. Close the lid and continue cooking for 3 more minutes for medium-rare. Discard the remaining basting butter.
8. Transfer the steaks to a platter and baste them with some of the garlic butter reserved for serving. Let the steaks rest for 5 minutes. Slice across the grain and serve with the remaining garlic butter.

Pumpkin Meatloaf With Pumpkin Bbq Sauce

Servings:12
Cooking Time: 70 Minutes

Ingredients:

- 4 pounds of ground beef
- 4 ounces bread crumbs (from about 3 slices of bread)
- 1 cup canned pumpkin
- 2 eggs
- 1 tsp kosher salt
- 1 tsp cinnamon
- 1 tsp chili powder
- 1 clove garlic
- 1/2 tsp smoked paprika (optional)
- 2 cups ketchup

- 1 cup canned pumpkin
- 2.5 tbsp water
- 2 tbsp apple cider vinegar
- 1.5 tbsp brown sugar
- 2 tsp cinnamon
- 1 tsp chili powder
- 1 tsp garlic powder
- 1 tsp smoked paprika (optional)

Dircctions:

1. Preheat the grill to 400°F using direct heat with a cast iron grate installed.
2. Combine all the ingredients into a large bowl (give yourself lots of room!) and mash, squeeze, and knead around until mixed thoroughly.
3. Spray your loaf pan and form the loaf inside.
4. Cook for about 70 minutes, or until inner temperature reaches 160°F.
5. Serve sauce over sliced meatloaf
6. Combine ingredients in a saucepan and heat on kamado grill until sauce is warm and thick.

Braised Short Ribs

Servings:8
Cooking Time: 130 Minutes

Ingredients:

- 8 bone-in beef short ribs
- 1 tsp salt
- 2 tsp freshly ground black pepper
- 4 tbsp olive oil
- ½ cup yellow onion, diced
- 3 cloves garlic, minced
- 1 cup beef broth
- 3 tbsp Worcestershire sauce
- 1 cup red wine

- 2 sprigs of rosemary

Directions:

1. Preheat the grill to 350°F using direct heat with a cast iron grate installed.
2. Season the short ribs with salt and pepper. Heat olive oil in the dutch oven. Sear short ribs for 1 minute per side. Remove from the dutch oven and set aside.
3. Add the onion to the dutch oven and cook for 3 minutes or until it is translucent. Add in garlic and cook for an additional minute.
4. Pour beef broth, Worcestershire sauce and red wine into the dutch oven. Bring to a simmer and add in the short ribs. Place the rosemary sprigs on top. Cover the dutch oven and cook for 2½ hours, or until meat is tender.

Grilled Meatloaf

Servings: 8
Cooking Time: 70 Minutes

Ingredients:

- 2lb (1kg) ground chuck
- 1lb (450g) ground pork
- 1 cup panko breadcrumbs
- 2 large eggs
- 2 sprigs of fresh thyme, leaves only
- kosher salt and freshly ground black pepper
- 8 bacon slices (not thick cut)
- olive oil
- for the relish
- 1 medium white onion, halved
- 3 red bell peppers, halved
- 2 tbsp extra virgin olive oil
- 3 garlic cloves, minced
- 3 bay leaves

- 3 tomatoes, seeded and finely diced
- 1/3 cup chopped fresh flat-leaf parsley
- 1 cup ketchup
- 41/2 tsp Worcestershire sauce
- kosher salt and freshly ground black pepper

Directions:

1. Preheat the grill to 400°F (204°C) using indirect heat with a cast iron grate and a cast iron skillet installed. Place onion and peppers on the grate (not in the skillet) and grill until beginning to soften and char, about 7 to 10 minutes. Remove the vegetables from the grill, dice the onion, and seed and dice the peppers.

2. To make the relish, in the hot skillet, heat oil until shimmering. Add onion, garlic, and bay leaves, and sauté for 2 to 3 minutes. Add peppers, and sauté for 2 to 3 minutes more, then add the tomatoes. Stir in parsley, ketchup, and Worcestershire sauce. Season with salt and pepper to taste. Simmer for 3 minutes, remove bay leaves, and remove the skillet from the grill. (You should have about 2 cups of relish.)

3. In a large bowl, combine ground beef, ground pork, breadcrumbs, eggs, thyme, and 1/2 cup relish. Season salt and pepper to taste. Form the meat mixture into a 9 x 4in (23 x 10cm) loaf. Lay bacon slices flat on a work surface, overlapping the long edges slightly to form a rectangle. Place the meatloaf crosswise on the bacon and bring the ends of the bacon strips up and around the meat so the meatloaf is fully wrapped in bacon.

4. Place the meatloaf seam side down in the center of the grill, close the lid, and grill until the internal temperature reaches160°F (71°C), about 30 to 45 minutes. Transfer the meatloaf to a serving platter and let cool completely.

5. Cut the cooled meatloaf into thick slices. Brush a small amount of oil on both sides of each slice, return to the grill, close the lid, and grill for 2 to 3 minutes per side. Serve immediately with the remaining relish, warmed on the stovetop (if desired).

Pastrami Beef Short Ribs

Servings:8
Cooking Time: 120 Minutes

Ingredients:

- 1 Whole Snake River Farms Beef Plate Short Rib
- Corning Brine
- Pastrami Rub
- 1 gallon water
- 1½ cups Kosher salt
- ¾ cups granulated sugar
- ¾ cups brown sugar
- 1 Tbsp + 2 tsp Tinted Cure Mix #1 (Pink Salt)
- 4 bay leaves, crushed
- 1 Tbsp juniper berries, crushed
- 10 cloves, whole
- 1 Tbsp black peppercorns, crushed
- 1 Tbsp coriander seeds, crushed
- 1 Tbsp mustard seeds
- 5 garlic cloves, crushed
- ¼ cup honey
- 1 cup black peppercorns, coarsely ground
- ½ cup coriander seeds, coarsely ground
- ½ cup onion powder
- ½ cup granulated garlic powder

- ¼ cup juniper berries, ground

Directions:

1. Combine all of the brine ingredients in a large pot and bring to a simmer. Simmer for 15 minutes, then cool and store overnight in the refrigerator. Place the whole short rib in a 2 gallon zipper bag. Then pour the cold brine in the bag. The bag should hold the full gallon of brine. Let the rib brine for a minimum of 48 hours. Flip the bag over each day.
2. Grind the peppercorns and coriander seeds in a mortar and pestle or a coffee grinder for the best results. Start with a full cup of each before you grind them. After grinding, combine the peppercorns and coriander seeds with the onion powder, garlic powder and the ground Juniper berries.
3. Remove the short rib from the brine. Pat dry with a paper towel. Liberally coat the rib with the pastrami rub. Do not be afraid to go heavy with this rub!
4. Preheat the grill to 275°F using direct heat with a cast iron grate installed.
5. Place the short ribs meat side up in the smoker. Smoke the ribs for two hours at 275°F. Next, reduce the temperature to 250°F. Smoke until the rib reaches an internal temperature of 185°F.
6. At this stage, wrap ribs in butcher's paper, or place in a large paper grocery bag. Once wrapped, place back in the smoker until the ribs reach an internal temperature of 203°F. Remove from the smoker and allow the rib to rest in the paper for 20-25 minutes before serving.

Texas-style Beef Brisket

Servings:12
Cooking Time: 360 Minutes

Ingredients:

- 1 whole brisket, about 12 pounds
- 2 tablespoons olive oil
- Classic Steakhouse Seasoning

Directions:

1. Preheat the grill to 275°F using direct heat with a cast iron grate installed.
2. With a sharp knife trim out some of the fat that is in between the two muscles of the brisket so it will cook evenly. Trim any extreme fat from the top, but most of it should remain. Rub the brisket all over with the oil, then season it liberally on all of the exposed meat using Classic Steakhouse Seasoning.
3. Place the brisket in the grill, fat side down, and cook for 6 hours. Flip to cook fat side up for another 2 hours. Lay out a large double thick sheet of heavy-duty aluminum foil or butcher paper. Lay the brisket on the foil or butcher paper fat side up and wrap. Return to the kamado grill and cook until the brisket reaches an internal temperature of 200°F deep in the thick part of the meat. This should take another 3 to 4 hours but be sure to check the temperature.
4. When the brisket reaches to the internal temperature of 200°F place it in an empty ice chest and let it rest for at least 15 minutes and up to 4 hours. Take the brisket out of the foil and place it on a cutting board. Reserve the juices. Trim away all of the excess fat. Slice the brisket through

both muscles across the grain and about 3/8" thick. With a spoon remove as much fat as possible from the juices, then drizzle over the top of the sliced brisket.

Reverse-seared Ribeye

Servings:6
Cooking Time: 50 Minutes

Ingredients:

- 5 lb. (2.25 kg) whole boneless ribeye
- ¼ cup (60 ml) salt
- ¼ cup (60 ml) pepper
- ¼ cup (60 ml) tarragon, finely chopped
- ¼ cup (60 ml) thyme, finely chopped
- ¼ cup (60 ml) parsley, finely chopped
- 1 lb salted butter, brought to room temperature

Directions:

1. Preheat the grill to 275°F using direct heat with a cast iron grate installed. (later in the cook we will remove the platesetter for direct cooking and stabilize at 600°F.)
2. Trim off any excess fat from the ribeye and then cut it into 4 to 5 – 2 inch (5 cm) thick steaks.
3. Combine the salt and pepper to create the Dalmatian rub and apply the rub to all sides of the steaks.
4. Combine the butter and herbs and massage about 1 tablespoon of the compound butter onto each steak. Roll the rest of the butter into a roll and chill.
5. Place the steaks on the cast iron grid and roast until they reach an internal temperature of 115°F, about 45 minutes.

Put the steaks aside and reset the kamado grill for direct cooking at 600°F.

6. Sear the steaks for 2 minutes per side, remove from the grill. Top each steak with about 1 tablespoon compound butter and rest for 10 minutes before serving.
7. Combine the salt and pepper to create the Dalmatian rub and apply the rub to all sides of the steaks.
8. Combine the butter and herbs and massage about 1 tablespoon of the compound butter onto each steak. Roll the rest of the butter into a roll and chill.

Pimento Cheeseburgers

Servings:4
Cooking Time: 20 Minutes

Ingredients:

- 1½ cups grated extra-sharp cheddar cheese
- ¼ cup maynnaise
- 2 tablespoons finely chopped roasted red pepper
- 1 teaspoon grated onion
- Pinch of cayenne

Directions:

1. Combine the grated cheese, mayonnaise, red pepper, onion, and cayenne in a small mixing bowl until well blended and creamy. Taste and if it needs a bit of salt, add a pinch. Cover and refrigerate the cheese spread until about 20 minutes before you're ready to use it. Grill burgers to your liking, then slide them to the outside edge of the cooking grid so that they don't overcook. Put 2 heaping tablespoon-sized dollops on

top, close the dome of the kamado grill and heat until melted.

Tex Mex Burger

Servings: 4
Cooking Time: 8 Minutes

Ingredients:
- 4 Nature's Own 100% Whole Wheat Sandwich Rolls 2 teaspoons fresh lime juice
- 1 teaspoon ground cumin
- 1 teaspoon chili powder
- 1/4 teaspoon salt
- 1/8 teaspoon black pepper
- Dash cayenne pepper
- 1 pound lean ground beef
- 4 slices Manchego, Chihuahua or Cheddar cheese 4 tablespoons sour cream
- Jalapeño pepper jelly

Directions:
1. Preheat the grill to 350°F using direct heat with a cast iron grate installed.
2. Combine lime juice, cumin, chili powder, salt, black pepper and cayenne pepper in a large bowl; mix well. Add beef; mix well. Form into 4 patties.
3. Cook about 4 minutes per side, adding cheese slices during the last 2 minutes of grilling.
4. Toast insides of sandwich rolls. Spread 1 tablespoon sour cream on each roll. Place burgers on roll bottoms. Garnish with jelly.

Smash Burgers

Servings: 16
Cooking Time: 8 Minutes

Ingredients:
- 2 tbsp unsalted butter
- 2 tbsp canola oil
- 1/2 cup minced shallots or red onion
- 2lb (1kg) ground chuck
- kosher salt and freshly ground black pepper
- 16 sweet Hawaiian rolls or slider buns
- 5oz (140g) Brie or cheese of choice, cut into 16 slices
- tomato slices, to serve
- dill pickle slices, to serve

Directions:
1. Preheat the grill to 400°F (204°C) using direct heat with a cast iron grate installed flat side up. To the hot griddle, add butter and canola oil. Make 8 small piles of half the shallots on the griddle, about 2 tsp per pile.
2. Portion ground beef into 16 balls, and season with salt and pepper to taste. Place one meatball on each pile of shallots. Using a spatula, smash the meat into the shallots, forming a thin patty.
3. Close the lid and grill the burgers until shallots begin to caramelize and the meat is cooked on the bottom, about 2 minutes. Don't move the patties. When the bottoms are caramelized, flip the burgers, being sure to get most of the shallots.
4. Place a slice of cheese on each patty and the top bun on the cheese. Leave in place on the griddle for 2 minutes. On a serving platter, top the bottom halves of the buns with tomato and pickle slices. Using a spatula, slide the burgers and top buns from the griddle and place atop the bottom buns. Repeat steps 2 through 4 with the

remaining shallots, meat, and toppings. Serve immediately.

Beef Barbacoa

Servings: 6
Cooking Time: 270 Minutes

Ingredients:

- 4lb (1.8kg) chuck-eye roast
- 2 bay leaves
- kosher salt and freshly ground black pepper
- 6 x 6-in (15.25-cm) corn tortillas, warmed
- for the sauce
- 2 tbsp vegetable oil
- 1 small white onion, finely sliced
- 6 garlic cloves, smashed
- 2 tsp ground cumin
- 1/2 tsp ground cloves
- 2 tsp dried oregano
- 4 chipotle peppers in adobo, roughly chopped, plus 2 tbsp adobo sauce
- 1/4 cup apple cider vinegar
- 4 cups low-sodium chicken stock, divided
- 1 dried New Mexico pepper, seeds and stem removed
- 1 dried ancho pepper, seeds and stem removed
- 1 dried negro pepper, seeds and stem removed
- 2 tsp fish sauce

Directions:

1. Preheat the grill to 375°F (191°C) using direct heat with nothing but coals in the grill. Place roast directly on the coals and sear all sides until browned and the internal temperature reaches 160°F (71°C), about 3 to 5 minutes per side. Remove roast from the grill and set aside.

2. Install the heat deflector and place a dutch oven on top. Close the top and bottom vents most of the way to lower the temperature to 325°F (163°C). To the hot dutch oven, add oil, onion, and garlic, and cook until onions are well browned, about 10 minutes. Add cumin, cloves, and oregano, and cook until fragrant, about 30 seconds, stirring constantly. Add chipotle peppers, adobo sauce, vinegar, and 2 cups stock to the dutch oven. Scrape up the browned bits from the bottom, and simmer until stock has reduced by about half, about 15 minutes. Transfer contents of the dutch oven to a blender and return the dutch oven to the grill.

3. Place dried peppers in a large saucepan and add remaining 2 cups chicken stock. Bring to a boil on the stovetop over high heat, reduce heat to low, and simmer until peppers are completely tender, about 15 minutes. Add the soaked peppers and their liquid to the blender with onion and chipotle mixture. Add the fish sauce. Purée until smooth, and set aside.

4. Place roast, bay leaves, and sauce in the dutch oven. Cook until the internal temperature reaches 185°F (85°C), about 4 hours, turning occasionally. Discard bay leaves. Transfer roast to a serving platter and cover with aluminum foil. Return the dutch oven to the grill and cook the remaining liquid until reduced to 11/2 cups, about 5 minutes, stirring frequently.

5. Roast can be cut and served immediately, but for the best flavor, place roast and sauce

in a sealable container and refrigerate for up to 5 days. When ready to serve, shred roast into chunks and transfer the meat and sauce to a large pot. On the stovetop over medium-high heat, bring to a simmer and cook, stirring gently, until beef is tender and coated in sauce, about 10 to 15 minutes.

Greek Lamb Stuffed Roma Tomatoes

Servings:4
Cooking Time: 7 Minutes

Ingredients:

- Cucumber Salsa
- Stuffing
- 1 Cup (240 ml) Cucumber (Chopped)
- 3 tbsp (45 ml) Onion (Chopped)
- 1 Clove Garlic (Chopped)
- 2 tbsp (30 ml) Dill (Chopped)
- 1 tbsp (15 ml) Greek Yogurt
- 1/2 tsp (3 ml) Lemon Juice
- Pinch of Salt and Ground Black Pepper
- 1 lb Ground Lamb
- 1/2 Large Onion (Chopped)
- 1 Portobello Mushroom (Chopped)
- 1 Clove Garlic
- 2 tbsp (30 ml) Olive Oil
- 1 tbsp (15 ml) Fresh Oregano
- 1 tbsp (15 ml) Rosemary
- 1/3 Cup (80 ml) Feta Cheese
- Pinch of Salt and Ground Black Pepper

Directions:

1. Combine all of the salsa ingredients and set aside until needed.

2. Preheat the grill to 350°F using direct heat with a cast iron grate installed.

3. Slice off the top of the tomatoes and scoop out the seeds and insides, being careful not to break the skin. Set upside-down on a paper towel to allow juices to run out for 10 minutes.

4. In a Stir Fry & Paella Pan, caramelize the onions. Brown the lamb with the salt and pepper. Add the mushrooms and 3 tablespoons of the tomato and cook for 1 minute. Add most of the feta cheese, reserving some for topping. Cook for 1 minute and remove from heat.

5. Place tomatoes on Grill Rings; fill tomatoes generously. Grill for 5-6 minutes or until tomato skins crack open slightly. Remove from heat, top with cucumber salsa and enjoy!

Taco Soup

Servings: 8
Cooking Time: 60 Minutes

Ingredients:

- 1 lb ground beef
- 4 cups chicken broth
- 1/2 cup chopped onion
- 1 Tablespoon garlic, minced
- 1 Tablespoon chili powder
- 1 Tablespoon smoked paprika
- 1 tsp ground cumin
- 2 cans pinto beans, rinsed and drained
- 1 can black beans, rinsed and drained
- 1 can corn, drained
- Salt & Pepper

Directions:

1. Place ingredients in a cold dutch oven and stir.
2. Grilling:
3. Preheat the grill to 350°F using direct heat with a cast iron grate installed.
4. Place the dutch oven on the grid of the grill and lower the dome for 1 hour.
5. Soup is done when the ground beef is cooked through.
6. Serve with shredded cheese, cut up avocado, shredded cabbage and tortilla chips.

Pastrami On Rye With Deli Mayo And Fresh Pickles

Servings:10
Cooking Time: 480 Minutes

Ingredients:
- 4½ lbs (2 kg) grassfed beef brisket – deboned, fat on
- Hickory chips for smoking
- 3 cups (.7 L) water
- ¼ cup (60 ml) kosher salt
- ¼ cup (60 ml) brown sugar
- 2 bay leaves
- 1 tbsp (15 ml) coriander seeds, crushed
- 1 tsp (5 ml) peppercorns, crushed
- 1 tbsp (15 ml) mustard seeds, crushed
- 4 tbsp (60 ml) fresh coarsely ground black pepper
- 2 tbsp (30 ml) coriander powder
- 1 tsp (5 ml) mustard powder
- 1 tbsp (15 ml) brown sugar
- 1 tbsp (15 ml) paprika
- 2 tsp (10 ml) garlic powder
- 2 tsp (10 ml) onion powder

Directions:
1. Place all ingredients in a pot and heat until sugar is dissolved. Using the Stainless Steel Flavor Injector, inject the pickling mix into the meat. Place the brisket in a deep dish, pour in the remaining pickling mix and cover dish with cling wrap. Place in the back of the refrigerator for 3 days. Nurse it by turning it every day and making sure the pickling covers the meat. After 3 days take it out and soak it for 8 hours in cold water. Pat dry.
2. Mix rub ingredients together. Massage a little oil onto the beef brisket to help the seasoning stick; rub spice mix generously onto the brisket and refrigerate to season overnight.
3. Preheat the grill to 215°F using direct heat with a cast iron grate installed. Add pre-soaked hickory wood chips and smoke the meat for 8 hours. The internal temperature should reach 145°F. Serve sandwiched between dark rye slices with sweet and sour pickles and a bit of deli mayo (mayo mixed with a little mustard).

DESSERTS

Bread Pudding

Servings: 8
Cooking Time: 60 Minutes

Ingredients:

- 1 1/2 cups milk
- 10 eggs
- 1 loaf French bread, cut into 1 1/2 inch cubes
- 1 1/2 cups sugar
- 1 cup raisins (optional)
- 2 Tablespoons vanilla
- 2 tsp cinnamon
- 1/2 tsp nutmeg
- 1/4 tsp salt

Directions:

1. Line the dutch oven with a liner.
2. Place bread cubes and raisins into the dutch oven.
3. In a large bowl, combine eggs, milk, sugar, vanilla, cinnamon, nutmeg, and salt.
4. Pour the mixture over the bread and raisins.
5. Allow the bread mixture to sit for 30 minutes.
6. Grilling:
7. Preheat the grill to 350°F using direct heat with a cast iron grate installed.
8. Cover the dutch oven, place it on the grid, and lower the dome for 1 hour.
9. Serve the bread pudding with vanilla ice cream or whipped cream.

S'mores Pizza

Servings: 8

Cooking Time: 5 Minutes

Ingredients:

- 1 pizza dough
- 1/2 cup semi-sweet chocolate chips
- 1/2 cup miniature marshmallows
- 1/4 cup slightly crushed graham crackers

Directions:

1. Stretch dough to a 14" round and place on a pizza peel.
2. Sprinkle dough with chocolate chips, miniature marshmallows, and graham cracker crumbs.
3. Grilling:
4. Slide the pizza onto the prepared stone at 500°F.
5. Cook for 5 minutes, remove from the stone, slice, and serve.

Buttermilk Biscuits

Servings: 6
Cooking Time: 15 Minutes

Ingredients:

- 3/4 cups buttermilk
- 1/2 cup butter, cut into 1/2 inch cubes
- 3 cups flour
- 1 1/2 tsp baking powder
- 1/2 tsp salt

Directions:

1. In the bowl of a food processor, combine flour, baking powder, salt and butter and pulse until the butter is the size of small peas.

2. With the food processor going, stream in buttermilk until the dough just comes together.
3. Turn out on a floured surface.
4. Pat the dough to 1/2-inch thickness and fold in half.
5. Pat the dough to 1/2-inch thickness and fold in half again.
6. Pat the dough a third time to 1/2-inch thickness.
7. Using a pizza cutter, cut the dough into 12 square biscuits.
8. Place a sheet of parchment in the bottom of the dutch oven.
9. Place biscuits on the bottom of the dutch oven, being careful that they do not touch. (You may have to do this in two batches.)
10. Grilling:
11. Preheat the grill to 425°F using direct heat with a cast iron grate installed.
12. Cover the dutch oven with the lid and place on the grid.
13. Lower the dome for 12-15 minutes.
14. Biscuits are done when they are golden brown. Serve with butter, honey, or jam.

Best Banana Bread

Servings: 6
Cooking Time: 40 Minutes

Ingredients:
- 1 cup plain yogurt
- 1/4 cup butter
- 3 very ripe bananas, peeled
- 2 eggs
- 2 cups flour
- 2/3 cups sugar
- 3/4 tsp salt

- 1/2 tsp vanilla extract
- 1/2 tsp baking soda
- 1/4 tsp baking powder

Directions:
1. In a blender, combine bananas, yogurt, sugar, butter, vanilla, and eggs until smooth.
2. In a large bowl, sift together flour, salt, baking powder, and baking soda.
3. Gradually add the wet ingredients into the dry ingredients and gently stir to combine. DO NOT OVER MIX.
4. Line a dutch oven with a liner.
5. Pour batter into the dutch oven and cover.
6. Grilling:
7. Preheat the grill to 350°F using direct heat with a cast iron grate installed and place the dutch oven on the grid.
8. Lower the dome for 30 minutes or until a toothpick inserted into the center comes out clean.

Orange Scented Vanilla Cake

Servings: 12
Cooking Time: 30 Minutes

Ingredients:
- 12 oranges
- 1/2 stick of butter
- 1 vanilla cake mix, prepared according to package instructions
- 1/2 lb of powdered sugar

Directions:
1. Cut the tops off of the oranges and, using a spoon, scoop out the insides of the orange. Eat the insides of the orange while you wait for the cake to cook.

2. Pour 1/3 of a cup of batter into each orange, replace the top and wrap with heavy duty aluminum foil.
3. In a separate bowl, combine butter, powdered sugar, and 2 Tablespoon orange juice.
4. When cakes are ready, drizzle some of the glaze over top of each cake and serve inside the orange.
5. Grilling:
6. Place the oranges on a 350°F grill for 30 minutes or until the cake is done.

Grilled Plums With Honey And Ricotta

Servings: 4
Cooking Time: 5 Minutes

Ingredients:
- 4 plums, cut in half and pitted
- 1/2 cup whole milk ricotta cheese
- 2 Tablespoons honey
- 1/4 tsp cracked black pepper

Directions:
1. Place the plums, cut side down on a 400°F grill.
2. Close the dome for 5 minutes.
3. Assembly:
4. Serve the plums, cut side up, with a dollop of ricotta, a drizzle of honey, and a sprinkling of cracked black pepper.

Brownies

Servings: 6
Cooking Time: 30 Minutes

Ingredients:

- 1 1/2 cups flour
- 1 cup white sugar
- 1 cup brown sugar
- 3/4 cups cocoa powder
- 1/2 cup butter, melted
- 1/4 cup vegetable oil
- 2 tsp vanilla
- 1 tsp baking powder
- 1/2 tsp salt
- 4 eggs
- 1/2 cup chocolate chips
- 1/2 chip marshmallows

Directions:
1. In a large bowl, combine butter, oil and sugars.
2. Add eggs, one at a time, stirring in between.
3. Add vanilla and stir.
4. Sift together cocoa powder, baking powder, and flour.
5. Add to the butter and egg mixture and stir until just combined.
6. Grilling:
7. Preheat the grill to 350°F using direct heat with a cast iron grate installed.
8. Line the dutch oven with a liner.
9. Pour the batter into the liner.
10. Cover the dutch oven, place on the grid, and lower the dome for 25-30 minutes or until a toothpick inserted into the middle comes out clean.
11. Remove the lid, top the brownies with chocolate chips and marshmallows and replace the lid for 5 minutes until the toppings are melted.

Almond Cream Cake

Servings: 16
Cooking Time: 45 Minutes

Ingredients:

- 2 cups butter, softened
- 3 cups sugar
- 6 cups cake flour
- 1 tsp kosher salt
- 4 tsp baking powder
- 2 cups whole milk
- 2 tsp almond extract
- 10 large eggs, whites only
- sliced almonds, to decorate
- for the frosting
- 1 1/4 cups all-purpose flour
- 2 cups whole milk
- 1/2 tsp almond extract
- 1 tbsp vanilla bean paste
- 2 cups butter, softened
- 2 cups sugar

Directions:

1. In the bowl of a stand mixer fitted with the paddle attachment, cream butter until white in appearance. Add sugar and beat until fluffy. In a large bowl, sift together flour, salt, and baking powder. Add the flour mixture to the butter mixture in three stages, alternating with the milk and almond extract and mixing after each addition until just combined.

2. In a large bowl, beat egg whites until they form stiff peaks. Using a spatula, gently fold egg whites into the cake batter, taking care not to overmix.

3. Preheat the grill to 350°F (177°C) using indirect heat with a standard grate installed.

Line an 11 x18-in (28 x 46cm) grill-safe baking pan with parchment paper and lightly grease with cooking spray. Pour the batter into the pan, place on the grate, close the lid, and bake until the top springs back when touched, about 27 to 30 minutes.

4. Remove the cake from the grill and place on a wire rack to cool for 10 minutes. Use a knife to loosen the edges, and transfer the cake to a wire rack to cool completely.

5. To make the frosting, on the stovetop in a saucepan over medium-low heat, whisk together flour and milk until mixture thickens to the consistency of mashed potatoes, about 12 to 15 minutes. Stir constantly, and lower the heat if needed. Remove the saucepan from the heat and place in a bowl of ice for 5 to 10 minutes to hasten the cooling process and bring the mixture to room temperature. Once cool, stir in almond extract.

6. In the bowl of a stand mixer, cream together vanilla paste, butter, and sugar until the mixture is light and fluffy and sugar is completely dissolved. Add the flour mixture, and beat until it has the appearance of whipped cream, scraping the sides of the bowl as needed.

7. Spread the frosting evenly over the cooled cake and sprinkle sliced almonds over top to decorate before serving.

Whole Apples With Caramel Sauce

Servings: 4
Cooking Time: 60 Minutes

Ingredients:

- 4 Jonathan Apples
- 1 cup packed dark brown sugar
- 1/2 cup half and half
- 4 Tablespoons butter
- 1 tsp vanilla extract

Directions:

1. In a medium saucepan, whisk together the brown sugar, butter, and half and half until melted.
2. Continue whisking 5-7 minutes until the caramel begins to thicken.
3. Add vanilla and set aside to cool before storing in a jar in the fridge.
4. Using a melon baller, scoop the core from the apple.
5. Wrap each apple in aluminum foil.
6. Grilling:
7. Preheat the grill to 225°F using direct heat with a cast iron grate installed for 1 hour.
8. Remove apples from the grill, serve topped with caramel sauce.

Apple Cake

Servings: 12
Cooking Time: 60 Minutes

Ingredients:

- 2 (21 oz) cans apple pie filling
- 1 (14 oz) jar caramel ice cream topping
- 1 box yellow cake mix, prepared according to package directions and mixed with 2 tsp cinnamon

Directions:

1. Prepare cake according to package directions.
2. Line a dutch oven with a liner.
3. Pour pie filling into the bottom of the dutch oven.
4. Top with caramel ice cream topping.
5. Top with prepared cake mix.
6. Grilling:
7. Preheat the grill to 350°F using direct heat with a cast iron grate installed.
8. Cover the dutch oven and place on the grid of the grill.
9. Lower the dome and cook for 1 hour.
10. Serve warm with whipped cream or ice cream.

Nutella And Strawberry Pizza

Servings: 8
Cooking Time: 5 Minutes

Ingredients:

- 1 pizza dough
- 1/2 lb sliced strawberries
- 1/4 cup Nutella

Directions:

1. Stretch the pizza dough into a 14 inch round and place it on a pizza peel.
2. Spread the dough with the Nutella and top with strawberries.
3. Grilling:
4. Slide the pizza onto the prepared stone in a 500°F grill and cook for 5 minutes.

5. Remove from the stone with a pizza peel and slice into 8 pieces.

Apple Pizza

Servings: 8
Cooking Time: 5 Minutes

Ingredients:
- 1 pizza dough
- 1 cup apple pie filling
- 1/4 cup vanilla cake mix
- 2 Tablespoon melted butter
- Vanilla Ice Cream

Directions:
1. Stretch pizza dough into a 14" round and place on a pizza peel.
2. In a small bowl, combine cake mix and melted butter until it forms a crumbly texture.
3. Spread apple pie filling over pizza dough and top with crumb mixture.
4. Grilling:
5. Bake on a pizza stone in a 500°F grill for 5 minutes.
6. Slice and serve with vanilla frosting.

Corn & Jalapeño Focaccia

Servings: 8
Cooking Time: 40 Minutes

Ingredients:
- 2½ cups all-purpose or bread flour
- 1 tbsp kosher salt
- ½ tbsp instant dry yeast
- 1½ cups warm water (105°F [41°C])
- 3 tbsp extra virgin olive oil
- 3 jalapeño peppers, left whole

- 1 ear of corn, shucked
- for the butter
- 1 tbsp olive oil
- 2 tbsp unsalted butter
- 4 garlic cloves, minced
- 2 tsp dried oregano
- ½ tsp red pepper flakes
- kosher salt

Directions:
1. In a large bowl, combine flour, salt, yeast, and water. Cover tightly with plastic wrap, and set aside to rest for at least 8 hours and up to 24 hours. The dough will rise dramatically and fill the bowl.
2. Pour oil into a large cast iron skillet. Transfer the dough to the skillet, turning the dough to coat in oil. Press the dough around the skillet, flattening slightly and spreading to fill the entire bottom. Cover tightly with plastic wrap and let sit at room temperature for 2 hours.
3. After the first hour, preheat the grill to 425°F (218°C) using indirect heat with a standard grate installed. Place jalapeños and corn on the grate near the edges. Close the lid and grill until beginning to soften and char, about 10 to 12 minutes. Cut the kernels from the cob, and seed and dice jalapeños. Set aside.
4. After resting for 2 hours, the dough should mostly fill the skillet. Use your fingertips to firmly press the dough to the edges, popping any large bubbles that appear. Lift the dough at the edges and allow any air bubbles underneath to escape.
5. Evenly scatter corn and jalapeños over the dough, then push down until they're

embedded in the dough. Place the skillet on the grate, close the grill lid, and bake until the top is golden brown and the bottom appears golden brown and crisp when lifted at the edge with a spatula, about 16 to 24 minutes.

6. To make the butter, on the stovetop in a small saucepan over medium-low heat, heat oil and butter until butter melts. Add garlic, oregano, and pepper flakes, and cook for 1 minute, stirring constantly. Transfer to a small bowl and season with salt to taste.

7. Transfer the focaccia to a cutting board and brush the butter over top. Allow to cool slightly, slice, and serve with any remaining butter.

Peach Dutch Baby

Servings: 8
Cooking Time: 25 Minutes

Ingredients:

- 8 oz frozen peaches, thawed (or 3 ripe peaches, peeled and sliced)
- 1 cup whole milk
- 4 eggs
- 1 cup flour
- 1/4 cup sugar
- 1/4 cup butter
- 1 tsp vanilla
- 1 tsp cinnamon
- 1/2 tsp salt

Directions:

1. In a blender, combine milk, flour, sugar, vanilla, cinnamon, salt, and eggs until smooth.
2. Grilling:

3. Preheat the grill to 425°F using direct heat with a cast iron grate installed.
4. Place the dutch oven on the grid of the grill and melt the butter.
5. Line the bottom of the pot with peaches and pour over milk and egg mixture.
6. Close the dome for 20 minutes or until the top of the Dutch Baby is golden brown.
7. Serve with a sprinkling of powdered sugar.

Chocolate Cake

Servings: 12
Cooking Time: 45 Minutes

Ingredients:

- 2 cups all-purpose flour
- 2 cups sugar
- 2/3 cup cocoa powder
- 2 tsp baking soda
- 1 tsp baking powder
- 1 tsp kosher salt
- 2 large eggs, at room temperature
- 1 cup buttermilk, at room temperature
- 1 cup strong black coffee, warm
- 1/2 cup vegetable oil
- 1 tbsp pure vanilla extract
- flaky sea salt, for topping (optional)
- for the caramel sauce
- 3/4 cup sugar
- 4 tbsp water
- 4 tsp light corn syrup
- 1/4 cup heavy cream
- 1 tsp pure vanilla extract
- 11/2 tbsp unsalted butter
- for the frosting
- 12 tbsp unsalted butter, at room temperature
- 21/2 cups powdered sugar
- 1 tsp pure vanilla extract

- 1 tbsp heavy cream
- kosher salt

Directions:

1. Preheat the grill to 350°F (177°C) using indirect heat with a standard grate installed. Grease a 9-in (23-cm) round metal cake pan with nonstick cooking spray and line with parchment paper. (Instead of a cake pan, you can also use a well-seasoned dutch oven.)

2. In a large bowl or the bowl of a stand mixer, sift together flour, sugar, cocoa powder, baking soda, baking powder, and salt. In a separate medium bowl, whisk together eggs, buttermilk, coffee, vegetable oil, and vanilla extract.

3. Gradually add the liquid ingredients to the dry ingredients, stopping to scrape the sides and bottom of the bowl, until just combined. (The batter will be thin.) Pour the batter into the prepared cake pan or dutch oven. Place on the grate, close the grill lid, and bake until a toothpick inserted in the center comes out almost clean, about 25 to 30 minutes. Let sit for 5 minutes, then turn out onto a wire rack to cool completely. (Use a butter knife to loosen the edges if needed.)

4. To make the caramel sauce, in a small saucepan, combine sugar, water, and corn syrup. Place on the stovetop over medium heat, and simmer until the mixture is deep amber in color, about 10 to 15 minutes. Slowly and carefully, add heavy cream, whisking constantly, then whisk in vanilla, butter, and a pinch of salt.

5. To make the frosting, in the bowl of a stand mixer fitted with the paddle attachment, beat butter on medium speed until light and fluffy, about 2 to 3 minutes. Add sugar, vanilla extract, heavy cream, and a pinch of salt. Beat on low speed until combined, about 1 minute. Increase the speed to medium-high and beat for 6 minutes. Add 1/2 cup caramel sauce and mix until combined.

6. Spread the frosting evenly over top and sides of the cooled cake, and drizzle with caramel sauce. Sprinkle with flaky sea salt (if desired) before serving.

4 Ingredient, No Knead Bread

Servings: 4
Cooking Time: 30 Minutes

Ingredients:

- 3 cups warm water
- 1 1/2 Tablespoons yeast
- 1 1/2 Tablespoons salt
- 6 1/2 cups bread flour

Directions:

1. In a 4-quart ice cream container, mix all ingredients until they come together. DO NOT KNEAD.

2. Cover, but do not seal the container and allow it to sit in a warm, dry place until it doubles in size, about 30 minutes.

3. Seal the container and place in the fridge for 1 hour.

4. Place a sheet of parchment paper in the bottom of the dutch oven.

5. Pinch off 1/4 of the dough and form into a ball.

6. Place the ball on the parchment paper and allow it to rest while the grill heats.
7. Grilling:
8. Preheat the grill to 425°F using direct heat with a cast iron grate installed.
9. Score the top of the dough ball with an "X".
10. Cover the dutch oven and place it on the grid of the grill.
11. Lower the Dome for 30 minutes.
12. Remove the bread from the dutch oven and allow it to cool before slicing.

Grilled Sopapillas

Servings: 6
Cooking Time: 18 Minutes

Ingredients:

- 1 pizza dough, divided into 6 pieces
- 3 Tablespoons melted butter
- 1/4 cup sugar
- 1 Tablespoon cinnamon

Directions:

1. Stretch dough into round shape.
2. Place the dough directly on the pizza stone in a 500°F grill.
3. Brush with melted butter and top with cinnamon sugar.
4. Close the dome for 3 minutes, then remove.
5. Repeat with remaining dough.

Grilled Pineapple Sundaes

Servings: 4
Cooking Time: 5 Minutes

Ingredients:

- 4 fresh pineapple spears
- Vanilla Ice Cream
- Jarred Caramel Sauce
- Toasted Coconut

Directions:

1. Place pineapple spears on a 400°F grill and close the dome for 2 minutes.
2. Turn the pineapple and close the dome for another 2 minutes.
3. Turn the pineapple once more and close the dome for another minute.
4. Assembly:
5. Serve pineapple topped with ice cream, caramel sauce, and toasted coconut.

Upside Down Triple Berry Pie

Servings: 8
Cooking Time: 35 Minutes

Ingredients:

- 6 cups frozen triple berry mix
- 2 Tablespoons lemon juice
- 1 refrigerated pie crust
- 1 cup sugar, divided
- 4 Tablespoons cornstarch

Directions:

1. Place a liner in the dutch oven.
2. In a separate bowl, combine frozen berries with 3/4 cup sugar, cornstarch, and lemon juice.
3. Pour berries into the bottom of the lined dutch oven.
4. Unroll pie crust and place on top of berry mixture.
5. Cut 4 vent holes into the crust.
6. Sprinkle remaining sugar over the pie crust.
7. Grilling:
8. Preheat the grill to 425°F using direct heat with a cast iron grate installed.

9. Cover the dutch oven and place on the grid.

10. Lower the dome for 35 minutes or until the crust is golden and the berry mixture has thickened.

11. Cut the crust as you would any pie.

12. Serve a piece of crust topped with ice cream and a scoop of the thickened berry mixture.

Seasonal Fruit Cobbler

Servings: 12
Cooking Time: 90 Minutes

Ingredients:

- 2lb (1kg) seasonal fruit, washed, pitted (if needed), and sliced or halved if needed
- ½ tsp ground cinnamon
- 2 tsp cornstarch (for juicy fruits; omit for pears or apples)
- 4 tbsp butter, plus more for greasing
- ½ cup sugar, plus more for sprinkling
- ¾ cup self-rising flour
- ¾ cup whole milk
- whipped cream, to serve

Directions:

1. Preheat the grill to 350°F (177°C) using indirect heat with a standard grate installed. Place the fruit on the grate (or in a cast iron skillet if the fruit might fall through the grate), close the lid, and grill until beginning to soften and char, about 7 to 10 minutes. Remove fruit from the grill and place in a large bowl. Sprinkle cinnamon and cornstarch (if using) over fruit, and add a little sugar (if desired). Gently toss to coat and set aside.

2. Grease a 9-in (23-cm) grill-safe baking pan with butter. On the stovetop in a small saucepan, heat 4 tbsp butter over medium-low heat until beginning to brown, about 10 to 15 minutes.

3. In a medium bowl, whisk together butter, sugar, flour, and milk. Transfer fruit to the prepared baking pan and spread the batter evenly over top. Place the pan on the grate, close the lid, and bake until golden brown and bubbly, about 1 hour. In the last 10 minutes of cooking, sprinkle a light amount of sugar over top. Remove the cobbler from the grill, and serve warm with whipped cream on top.

Peaches And Pound Cake

Servings: 6
Cooking Time: 5 Minutes

Ingredients:

- 1/2 cup heavy whipping cream
- 2 Tablespoons sour cream
- 3 peaches, halved and pitted
- 1 store-bought pound cake, cut into 6 slices

Directions:

1. Place the peaches, cut side down, on a 400°F grill.

2. Place the pound cake slices alongside the peaches and close the dome for 2 minutes.

3. Flip the pound cake, and close the dome for an additional 2-3 minutes.

4. Assembly:

5. In a stand mixer, whip the whipping cream until stiff peaks form. Fold in the sour cream to combine.

6. Place a slice of pound cake on a plate, top with a peach half, and a dollop of the cream.

Chocolate Chip Cookie Peanut Butter Cup S'mores

Servings: 4
Cooking Time: 5 Minutes

Ingredients:

- 8 chocolate chip cookies
- 4 peanut butter cup candies
- 4 marshmallows

Directions:

1. On the grid of a 225°F grill, place one cookie, flat side up, with one peanut butter cup candy and one marshmallow on top.
2. Close the dome for 5 minutes or until the marshmallow begins to puff.
3. Assembly:
4. Close the s'more with the other chocolate chip cookie and get ready for the sugar rush.

Triple Berry Crostata

Servings: 8
Cooking Time: 50 Minutes

Ingredients:

- 1 1/2 cups all-purpose flour
- 11 Tablespoons butter, cut into 1/2 inch cubes
- 3 Tablespoons whole milk
- 2 tsp sugar
- 1 large egg yolk
- 2 cups frozen triple berry blend
- 1/4 cup sugar
- 2 Tablespoons cornstarch

Directions:

1. In a food processor, combine flour and butter and pulse until pea-sized cubes of butter can be seen throughout the flour.
2. Add sugar, egg yolk, and milk and pulse until the dough comes together.
3. Form the dough into a circle, cover tightly with plastic wrap, and refrigerate 20 minutes.
4. Roll the dough into a large round and place on a pizza peel covered in cornmeal.
5. In a bowl, combine fruit, sugar, and cornstarch and pile into the center of the dough.
6. Beginning on one side, fold the dough 1/3 of the way over the fruit, repeating until a free-form tart is formed.
7. Grilling:
8. Preheat the grill to 350°F using direct heat with a cast iron grate installed.
9. Slide the crostata onto the pizza stone and close the dome for 40-55 minutes or until the crust is golden brown.
10. Remove the crostata from the grill and allow to cool slightly before slicing and serving.

Death By Chocolate

Servings: 8
Cooking Time: 60 Minutes

Ingredients:

- 1 chocolate cake mix, prepared according to package directions
- 2 cups chocolate chips
- 1 cup brown sugar
- 1 1/2 cups water
- 1/2 cup cocoa powder
- 1 (10 oz) bag miniature marshmallows

Directions:

1. Prepare cake mix according to package instructions.
2. Line the dutch oven with a liner.
3. In a medium bowl, combine water, brown sugar, and cocoa powder.
4. Pour the mixture into the bottom of the dutch oven.
5. Top with miniature marshmallows
6. Pour prepared cake mix on top.
7. Top with chocolate chips.
8. Grilling:
9. Preheat the grill to 350°F using direct heat with a cast iron grate installed.
10. Place the lid on the dutch oven and set on the grid of the grill.
11. Close the dome for 1 hour.
12. Remove the dutch oven from the grill, uncover, and serve warm.

Grilled Watermelon With Honey Yogurt

Servings: 4
Cooking Time: 4 Minutes

Ingredients:

- 1 round of watermelon, 1 inch thick
- 1/2 cup Greek-style yogurt
- 1 Tablespoon honey
- 1/4 tsp vanilla

Directions:

1. Place the watermelon on a 400°F grill with the dome down for 1 minute.
2. Turn the watermelon and lower the dome for an additional minute.
3. Assembly:

4. Cut the watermelon in quarters and place each on a small plate.
5. In a small bowl, combine yogurt, honey, and vanilla and spoon equal amounts over the watermelon. Serve.

Berry Upside-down Cake

Servings: 10
Cooking Time: 30 Minutes

Ingredients:

- 10 tbsp unsalted butter, at room temperature, divided
- 1 cup packed light brown sugar, divided
- 11oz (315g) fresh seasonal berries
- 1 large egg
- 1 tsp pure vanilla extract
- 2/3 cup sour cream
- 11/3 cups all-purpose flour
- 1 tbsp baking powder
- 1/4 tsp baking soda
- 1/2 tsp kosher salt
- 1/4 tsp ground cinnamon
- fresh mint leaves, to garnish
- whipped cream, to serve

Directions:

1. Preheat the grill to 350°F (177°C) using indirect heat with a standard grate installed and a cast iron skillet on the grate. Melt 2 tbsp butter in the skillet and swirl to coat. Remove the skillet from the grill. Sprinkle 1/3 cup brown sugar over butter, pour in berries, and shake the skillet until berries are evenly spread out. Set aside.
2. In the bowl of a stand mixer fitted with the paddle attachment, cream together remaining 8 tbsp butter and 2/3 cup brown

sugar until fluffy. Add egg, vanilla, and sour cream, and beat to combine.

3. In a medium bowl, sift together flour, baking powder, baking soda, salt, and cinnamon. Gradually add the dry ingredients to the butter and egg mixture until just incorporated. (The batter will be thick.) Using a rubber spatula, scoop the batter into the skillet, smoothing it over berries.

4. Place the skillet on the grate, close the lid, and bake until golden brown and a cake tester inserted into the middle of the cake comes out clean, about 30 minutes. Remove the skillet from the grill and place on a wire rack to cool for 15 minutes.

5. To serve, flip the cake upside down on a large serving platter and release from the skillet, leaving the berries on top. Garnish with fresh mint leaves, and serve with a dollop of whipped cream.

Caramel Cinnamon Rolls

Servings: 4
Cooking Time: 30 Minutes

Ingredients:

- 18 frozen cinnamon rolls, thawed (you can also used canned cinnamon rolls)
- 1/2 cup brown sugar
- 1/2 cup graham cracker crumbs
- 1/2 cup caramel ice cream topping
- 1 tsp cinnamon

Directions:

1. Line the dutch oven with a liner.

2. Cut each cinnamon roll into 4 pieces and arrange them around the bottom of the dutch oven.

3. In a separate bowl, combine brown sugar, graham cracker crumbs, and cinnamon.

4. Sprinkle some of the mixture over the layer of cinnamon rolls. Repeat.

5. Grilling:

6. Preheat the grill to 350°F using direct heat with a cast iron grate installed.

7. Cover the dutch oven and place it on the grid of the grill.

8. Lower the dome for 25-30 minutes or until the cinnamon rolls are golden brown.

9. Drizzle caramel ice cream topping over the warm rolls and serve.

Grilled Naan

Servings: 24
Cooking Time: 6 Minutes

Ingredients:

- 1 cup warm water (105°F [41°C])
- 1/4oz (7g) active dry yeast
- 1/4 cup sugar
- 3 tbsp whole milk
- 1 large egg, beaten
- 2 tsp kosher salt
- 20 1/4oz (575g) bread flour, plus more for kneading
- vegetable oil, for greasing
- 1/4 cup butter, melted

Directions:

1. In a large bowl, combine water and yeast. Let sit until frothy, about 10 minutes. Stir in sugar, milk, egg, salt, and flour to make a

soft dough. Knead on a lightly floured surface until smooth.

2. Lightly oil a large bowl, place the dough in the bowl, and cover with a damp cloth. Let sit to rise until the dough has doubled in volume, about 1 hour.

3. Punch the dough down and divide it into 4 balls (about the size of golf balls). Cover with a towel and allow to rise until the balls have doubled in size, about 30 minutes.

4. Preheat the grill to 425°F (218°C) using direct heat with a cast iron grate installed. Use a rolling pin one ball of dough into a thin circle. Lightly oil the grate, place the circle of dough on the grate, close the lid, and bake until puffy and lightly browned, about 2 to 3 minutes. Brush the uncooked side with butter, then flip the dough over and brush the cooked side with butter. Cook until puffy and lightly browned, about 3 minutes more. Repeat the cooking process with the remaining dough. (You can also bake all 4 balls at the same time.)

5. Remove the naan from the grill and sprinkle with seasoning of choice (if desired). Serve warm.

Banana Boats

Servings: 4
Cooking Time: 10 Minutes

Ingredients:
- 4 green bananas
- Chocolate chips
- Miniature marshmallows
- Peanut butter chips
- Crushed cookies

Directions:
1. Split a banana lengthwise from end to end leaving the peel intact on the opposite side.
2. Top with desired toppings.
3. Wrap the banana in heavy duty aluminum foil.
4. Grilling:
5. Preheat the grill to 425°F using direct heat with a cast iron grate installed and close the dome for 10 minutes.
6. Unwrap and serve topped with vanilla ice cream, whipped cream, or by themselves

Peanut Butter Bacon Bars

Servings: 8
Cooking Time: 25 Minutes

Ingredients:
- 1 package peanut butter cookie mix
- 1/2 cup chopped peanuts
- 1/2 cup bacon, cooked and crumbled
- 1/3 cup vegetable oil
- 1 egg
- 1 cup semi-sweet chocolate chips
- 1/2 cup bacon, cooked and crumbled

Directions:
1. Combine cookie mix, vegetable oil, egg, bacon, and peanuts and press into a lined dutch oven.
2. Grilling:
3. Preheat the grill to 350°F using direct heat with a cast iron grate installed.
4. Cover the dutch oven and place on the grid.
5. Lower the dome for 25 minutes.
6. Remove the lid and top with chocolate chips.

7. Replace the cover for 5 minutes until the chocolate chips are melted.
8. Spread the chocolate over the bars to coat them evenly.
9. Top with remaining bacon.
10. Allow the bars to cool before cutting.

Lemon Poppy Seed Cake

Servings: 10
Cooking Time: 45 Minutes

Ingredients:
- 1 tsp poppy seeds
- 2 lemons, zested and juiced
- 1 vanilla cake mix prepared according to package directions, substituting melted butter for oil and buttermilk for water
- 1 lb powdered sugar
- 4 ounces cream cheese
- 1 stick butter, softened
- 1/2 tsp vanilla
- 1/2 tsp lemon extract
- The juice and zest of 1 lemon

Directions:
1. Prepare cake mix according to package directions, substituting melted butter for the oil and buttermilk for the water.
2. Add the lemon zest, lemon juice, and poppy seeds.
3. Line the dutch oven with a liner.
4. Pour prepare cake mix into the liner and cover.
5. Grilling:
6. Preheat the grill to 350°F using direct heat with a cast iron grate installed.
7. Place the dutch oven on the grid and lower the dome for 30-40 minutes or until a toothpick inserted into the center comes out clean.
8. Meanwhile, combine glaze ingredients, adding milk to thin out the glaze if necessary.
9. Remove the cake from the grill and set aside to cool for 10 minutes before pouring glaze over the cake.
10. Serve warm.

Fresh Peach Crisp

Servings: 4
Cooking Time: 5 Minutes

Ingredients:
- 2 peaches, halved with pits removed
- Vanilla Ice Cream
- 1 cup good quality granola

Directions:
1. Grilling:
2. Place the peach halves, cut side down, on a 400°F grill and cover with the dome for 5 minutes.
3. Assembly:
4. Remove the peaches and place them, cut side up, in a bowl. Top with vanilla ice cream and granola.

Pizza Margherita

Servings: 2
Cooking Time: 6 Minutes

Ingredients:
- cornmeal, for dusting
- 1/4 cup marinara sauce
- 2oz (55g) fresh mozzarella, sliced
- 3 garlic cloves, thinly sliced

- 12–16 fresh basil leaves
- kosher salt and freshly ground black pepper
- grated Parmesan, to serve
- for the dough
- 12oz (340g) Italian 00 flour, plus more for dusting
- 4 tsp kosher salt
- 2 tsp instant dry yeast
- 6½oz (190ml) warm water (105°F [41°C])

Directions:

1. To make the dough, in a large bowl, whisk together flour, salt, and yeast until well combined. Add water, and use your hands to mix until no dry flour remains. Cover tightly with plastic wrap and allow to rise at room temperature for 2 to 4 hours. Turn the dough out onto a lightly floured surface and allow to sit at room temperature for 2 hours before baking.

2. Preheat the grill to 600°F (316°C) using indirect heat with a pizza stone resting directly on the heat deflector. (The pizza stone should be level with the grill rim.)

3. On a lightly floured work surface, roll out the dough to ¼ in (.5cm) thick and a 10-in (25cm) diameter. Lightly dust a pizza paddle or unrimmed baking sheet with cornmeal, and place the dough on top. Evenly spread the sauce over the dough, working from the center to the edges. Top with the sliced mozzarella and garlic.

4. Carefully slide the pizza from the paddle to the hot pizza stone. Close the lid and bake until the crust is golden brown and the cheese is melted and beginning to bubble, about 4 to 6 minutes.

5. Use the pizza paddle to remove the pizza from the grill. Scatter the basil leaves over top and sprinkle with salt, pepper, and Parmesan.

Sourdough Baguette

Servings: 4
Cooking Time: 25 Minutes

Ingredients:

- cornmeal, for dusting
- for Day 1 (starter)
- 8oz (225g) whole rye flour
- 8oz (235ml) warm water (105°F [41°C])
- for Day 2
- 8oz (225g) bread flour
- for Day 3
- 12oz (340g) bread flour
- 6oz (177ml) warm water (105°F [41°C])
- 8oz (225g) starter
- for Day 4
- 3oz (85g) whole rye flour
- 31oz (915ml) warm water (105°F [41°C])
- 9½oz (270g) starter
- 42oz (1.2kg) bread flour
- 3oz (85g) whole wheat flour
- 1oz (25g) kosher salt

Directions:

1. On Day 1, in a large bowl, combine flour and water, cover tightly with plastic wrap, and let sit overnight on the counter at warm room temperature, about 70°F (21°C). (Cooler temperatures might inhibit the growth of the starter.)

2. On Day 2, add flour to the starter and mix until a stiff, thick dough forms. Cover tightly with plastic wrap and let sit

overnight on the counter at warm room temperature. The dough will rise overnight.

3. On Day 3, in a large bowl, combine flour, water, and 8 ounces (225g) of the starter, and mix until a stiff, thick dough forms. Cover tightly with plastic wrap and let sit overnight on the counter at warm room temperature. The dough will rise overnight and should begin to smell yeasty. (Freeze remaining starter for later use.)

4. On Day 4, preheat the grill to 400°F (204°C) using indirect heat with a standard grate installed and a pizza stone on the grate. In a large bowl, combine rye flour, water, 9½ ounces (270g) of the starter, bread flour, wheat flour, and salt, and mix until a dough forms. Cover tightly with plastic wrap and let sit for 20 minutes on the counter. The dough will continue to smell yeasty. (Freeze remaining starter for later use.)

5. Form the dough into 4 baguette shapes that are 10 to 12 inches (25cm to 30.5cm) long and about 2½ inches (6.25cm) around. Make 3 slits in the top of each loaf to allow steam to escape. Sprinkle the pizza stone with cornmeal and place the loaves on the pizza stone. Close the lid and bake until the bread reaches an internal temperature of 190°F (88°C), about 20 to 25 minutes.

6. Remove the baguettes from the grill, place on a cutting board, and let rest before slicing and serving as desired.

Grilled Fruit Pie

Servings: 8
Cooking Time: 55 Minutes

Ingredients:

- for the crust
- 1 cup all-purpose flour, plus extra for rolling dough
- ½ tsp kosher salt
- ½ cup butter, chilled and cut into small cubes
- ¼ cup ice water
- 2lb (1kg) dried beans, for blind baking
- powdered sugar, for dusting
- whipped cream or ice cream, to serve (optional)
- for the filling
- 1¼lb (565g) seasonal fruit, such as pears and plums, halved and pitted
- ½ cup sugar
- 4 tbsp cornstarch
- 2 tbsp lemon juice

Directions:

1. Preheat the grill to 350°F (177°C) using indirect heat with a standard grate installed. Place fruit on the grate skin side up, keeping them toward the edges of the grate. Close the lid and grill until beginning to soften, about 3 to 5 minutes. Transfer to a cutting board and slice. Set aside.

2. To make the crust, in a food processor, combine flour and salt, pulsing 3 to 4 times. Add butter, and pulse until the texture is mealy, about 5 to 6 times. With the food processor running, slowly add the ice water in 1 tbsp increments until the dough comes together.

3. Turn out the dough onto a floured work surface and sprinkle with flour. Using a rolling pin, roll dough out to a 10- to 11-in (25- to 28-cm) circle. Carefully transfer the dough to a 9-in (23-cm) metal pie pan,

pressing the dough to the edges. Trim any overhang and crimp the edges. Prick the dough with a fork to prevent bubbles during baking. Place the pan in the fridge to chill for 15 minutes.

4. Spread a large piece of parchment paper over the dough and fill the pan with dry beans, pressing them into the edges of the dough. Place the pan on the grate, close the lid, and bake for 10 minutes. Remove the parchment and beans from the pan, and continue baking the crust until golden brown in color, about 10 to 15 minutes more. Remove the pan from the grill and let the crust cool completely before filling.

5. To make the filling, in a large bowl, combine sugar, cornstarch, and juice. Add the grilled fruit and toss lightly to coat. Pour the fruit mixture into the baked crust. Place on the grate, close the lid, and bake until the filling is thickened and bubbling at the edges, about 30 minutes.

6. Remove the pie from the grill and place on a wire rack to cool. Just before serving, sprinkle with powdered sugar. Serve with whipped cream or ice cream (if desired).

3 Ingredient Fruit Cobbler

Servings: 8
Cooking Time: 30 Minutes

Ingredients:
- 1 stick butter, sliced
- 2 (29 oz) cans fruit, drained but reserving 1/2 cup of the liquid
- 1 yellow cake mix

Directions:
1. Line the dutch oven with a liner
2. Pour fruit into the bottom of the dutch oven with 1/2 cup of reserved liquid
3. Sprinkle the top with cake mix
4. Dot the top with butter.
5. Grilling:
6. Preheat the grill to 350°F using direct heat with a cast iron grate installed.
7. Cover the dutch oven and place on the grid of the grill.
8. Lower the dome for 30 minutes.
9. Allow the cobbler to sit for 10 minutes off the heat before serving.

BURGERS

Breakfast Burger

Servings: 4
Cooking Time: 13 Minutes

Ingredients:
- 1 1/2 lb ground beef
- 1/2 lb ground pork breakfast sausage
- 2 Tablespoon butter
- 8 strips bacon
- 4 slices sharp cheddar cheese
- 4 Brioche buns
- 4 eggs
- 4 thick slices tomato

Directions:
1. In a medium bowl, mix ground beef and sausage until just combined.
2. Form into 4 patties and refrigerate while the grill heats.
3. Melt butter in a large skillet and fry the eggs for 2 minutes on each side.
4. Grilling:
5. Preheat the grill to 400°F using direct heat with a cast iron grate installed.
6. Place bacon on a small cookie sheet and place on the grid in the grill. Cook until crispy.
7. Place the patties on the grid and close the dome for 3 minutes.
8. Flip the burgers and replace the dome for an additional 3 minutes.
9. Close all of the vents and allow the burgers to sit for an additional 5 minutes. The internal temperature of the burger should be 150°F.
10. Place cheese on top of the burgers and cover for 1 more minute.
11. Assemble the burgers by placing a burger on the bottom bun, topping with bacon, tomato, and a fried egg.

Classic American Burger

Servings: 4
Cooking Time: 12 Minutes

Ingredients:
- 2 lbs ground beef
- 1/2 tsp salt
- 1/4 tsp pepper
- 4 slices American cheese
- 4 hamburger buns
- Green Leaf Lettuce
- Sliced Tomato
- Ketchup
- Mustard
- Sliced Pickle

Directions:
1. Form ground beef into four patties and season both sides with salt and pepper.
2. Grilling:
3. Preheat the grill to 500°F using direct heat with a cast iron grate installed.
4. Place burgers on the grid and close the dome for 3 minutes.
5. Flip burgers and close the dome for 2 more minutes.
6. Close all of the vents and allow the burgers to sit for 5 minutes.
7. Top each burger with a slice of cheese and close the dome for 1 more minute.

8. Build burgers with lettuce, tomato, pickle, mustard, and ketchup.

Oahu Burger

Servings: 4
Cooking Time: 12 Minutes

Ingredients:
- 2 lbs ground beef
- 1/4 cup thickened Teriyaki Marinade
- 1/4 cup mayonnaise
- 1/2 tsp sambal or sriracha
- 4 slices fresh pineapple, cored
- 4 slices tomato
- 4 slices butter lettuce
- 4 Hawaiian hamburger buns

Directions:
1. Form ground beef into four patties and season both sides with salt and pepper.
2. In a small bowl, mix mayonnaise with hot chile sauce and spread on buns.
3. Top each bun with a burger, slice of pineapple, lettuce and tomato.
4. Grilling:
5. Preheat the grill to 500°F using direct heat with a cast iron grate installed.
6. Place burgers on the grid and close the dome for 3 minutes.
7. Flip burgers, baste with Teriyaki Marinade, and place the pineapple slices on the grid. Close the dome for 2 more minutes.
8. Flip the burgers again and baste with remaining Teriyaki Marinade. Close the dome.
9. Close all of the vents and allow the burgers to sit for 5 minutes.

Quesadilla Burger

Servings: 4
Cooking Time: 12 Minutes

Ingredients:
- 2 lbs ground beef
- 2 Tablespoons Adobo Rub
- 1 cup shredded cheddar cheese
- 4 large flour tortillas
- Sour Cream
- Guacamole
- Salsa

Directions:
1. Form ground beef into four patties and season both sides with Adobo Rub.
2. Serve each burger with sour cream, guacamole, and salsa.
3. Grilling:
4. Preheat the grill to 500°F using direct heat with a cast iron grate installed.
5. Place burgers on the grid and close the dome for 3 minutes.
6. Flip burgers and close the dome for 2 more minutes.
7. Close all of the vents and allow the burgers to sit for 5 minutes.
8. Remove burgers and place flour tortillas on the grid.
9. Top each tortilla with shredded cheese and close the dome for 1 minute until the cheese melts.
10. Place a hamburger in the center of each tortilla and begin folding the tortilla around the burger like an envelope.

The Crowned Jewels Burger

Servings: 4
Cooking Time: 12 Minutes

Ingredients:

- 2 lbs ground beef
- 1/2 tsp salt
- 1/4 tsp pepper
- 1 lb thinly sliced pastrami
- 1 cup shredded Romaine lettuce
- 1/4 cup mayonnaise
- 2 Tablespoons ketchup
- 1/8 tsp onion powder
- 4 slices Sharp Cheddar cheese
- 4 hamburger buns
- 1 tomato, sliced

Directions:

1. Form ground beef into four patties and season both sides with salt and pepper.
2. Meanwhile, mix together mayonnaise, ketchup, and onion powder. Smear on each bun.
3. Place each pastrami and cheese covered burger on the prepared buns and top with shredded lettuce and tomato.
4. Grilling:
5. Preheat the grill to 500°F using direct heat with a cast iron grate installed.
6. Place burgers on the grid and close the dome for 3 minutes.
7. Flip burgers and close the dome for 2 more minutes.
8. Close all of the vents and allow the burgers to sit for 5 minutes.
9. Top each burger with 1/4 of the pastrami and a slice of cheese and close the dome for 1 more minute.

"the Masterpiece"

Servings: 4
Cooking Time: 12 Minutes

Ingredients:

- 2 lbs ground beef
- 6 ounces sliced mushrooms
- 4 Tablespoons shredded smoked Gouda
- 2 Tablespoons butter
- 2 Tablespoons olive oil
- 2 Tablespoons Dijon mustard
- 1/2 tsp salt
- 1/4 tsp pepper
- 8 slices bacon, cooked and crumbled
- 4 slices Swiss cheese
- 4 brioche buns
- 1 small onion, sliced

Directions:

1. Heat a skillet over medium heat and add 1 Tablespoon butter and 1 Tablespoon olive oil.
2. Place mushrooms in the pan and DO NOT MOVE THEM. Saute for 5-7 minutes or until the mushrooms are browned. Remove from the pan and set aside.
3. In the same skillet, heat remaining butter and olive oil and add onions. Saute over medium heat until they become translucent and begin to brown, about 10 minutes. Remove from the heat and set aside to cool.
4. Mix onion, mushrooms, and crumbled bacon.
5. Grilling:
6. Preheat the grill to 425°F using direct heat with a cast iron grate installed.
7. Form ground beef into eight patties and season both sides with salt and pepper.

8. Place a generous spoonful of the mushroom and onion mixture in the center of four patties and top with smoked Gouda.

9. Top with additional patty and press sides to seal the mixture inside.

10. Place burgers on the grid and close the dome for 5 minutes.

11. Flip burgers and close the dome for 3 more minutes.

12. Close all of the vents and allow the burgers to sit for 5 minutes.

13. Top each burger with a slice of Swiss cheese and close the dome for 1 more minute.

14. Spread buns with mustard, top with burgers and bun tops.

RECIPES INDEX

Porchetta 83

Pork Belly Burnt Ends 82

Pork Cacciatore 96

Pork Lettuce Wraps 85

Pork Rib Roast Roulade 105

Pork Tenderloin Sliders 86

Potato, Squash, And Tomato Gratin 12

Prosciutto And Pear Bruschetta 10

Prosciutto Wrapped Cheese Dogs 93

Pumpkin Meatloaf With Pumpkin Bbq Sauce 122

Q
Quesadilla Burger 150

R
Ratatouille 25

Ray's Herb Butter Prime Rib 110

Red Chili Scallops 70

Red Fish Pot Pie 57

Reverse Seared Ribeyes 112

Reverse-sear Ribeye 110

Reverse-seared Herb Crusted Bone-in Iberico Pork Loin 90

Reverse-seared Ribeye 126

Ricky Taylor's Peri Peri Lobster 71

Roasted Ham With Coca-cola Mustard Glaze 98

Roasted Potatoes 15

Rosemary Ranch Chicken Kebabs 38

S
S'mores Pizza 131

Scallops With Pea-sto 65

Seared Bison Filet 114

Seared Duck 103

Seasonal Fruit Cobbler 140

Sesame Prawns 58

Short Ribs & Polenta 115

Shrimp Burgers With Remoulade 71

Sloppy Joes 113

Smash Burgers 127

Smash Cheese Burgers 117

Smoked Andouille & Crawfish Gumbo 91

Smoked Beef Brisket 120

Smoked Beef Tenderloin 112

Smoked Brisket 107

Smoked Chicken Sandwich With Chipotle Mayonnaise 51

Smoked Goat Bolognese 111

Smoked King Salmon 60

Smoked Potato Salad 24

Smoked Scallops 72

Smoked Spicy Korean Spare Ribs 103

Smoked Turkey 54

Smoked Wings With Moonshine White Sauce And Ranch Pickles 35

Smoke-roasted Florida Oysters And Clams 72

Smokey Thai Pulled Chicken Sandwiches 34

Smoky Grilled Chicken Wings 41

Smoky Thai Pulled Chicken Sandwiches 39

Soba Noodle Bowl 20

Sourdough Baguette 146

Southwest Turkey Burgers 50

Spice-crusted Salmon With Rosé-glazed Vegetables 77

Spicy Bourbon Barrel Bbq Wings 43

Sriracha Pork Chops 82

Stuffed Chicken Breasts With Sundried Tomatoes And Artichokes 52

Summer Squash & Eggplant 9

Surf And Turf Rolls 108

Surf Perch 63

Sweet Potato Bake 20

Sweet Potato Fries 13

Swordfish Steaks With Peach Salsa 69

T
Taco Soup 129

Tex Mex Burger 127

Texas-style Beef Brisket 125

Thai Stuffed Chicken Drumsticks 37

Thanksgiving Stuffing 26

The Best Turkey Burger Ever 49

The Crowned Jewels Burger 151

The Perfect Roasted Turkey 31

Triple Berry Crostata 141

Turkey & Wild Mushroom Pot Pie 53

Turkey Bacon Dogs 104

Tyler Farr's Venison Cube Steak 118

U

Upside Down Triple Berry Pie 139

V
Venison Casserole 114

Vidalia Onion And Sriracha-glazed Nashville Hot Wings 35

W
Whole Apples With Caramel Sauce 135

Whole Grilled Snapper In Pipian Sauce 67

Whole Smoked Barbecue Chicken 40

Wickles Brine Blasted Chicken 42

Wild Mushroom And Blue Cheese Stuffed Burger 118

Wood-plank Loaded Mashed Potatoes 14

Wood-plank Stuffed Tomatoes 12

X
X Factor Chicken Steaks With Whiskey Grilled Onions 44

Z
Zesty Cedar Planked Cod 57

Printed in Great Britain
by Amazon